LOVING LOTTIE

How a Broken Romanian Dog Came to Britain
and Found Happiness

Hereford Books

Dedicated to,
and in recognition of the work of:

Blue Cross
Dogs Trust
PDSA
RSPCA
Scottish SPCA

Foreword

I started to write this book because I had fairly recently left Lottie with my future ex-wife and I couldn't get her out of my mind (Lottie not my wife). I am an author, and I thought that if I put my thoughts down on paper, or what passes for paper nowadays, I might exorcise her ghost, so to speak.

I stopped, after a while, because I felt it was a self-indulgent exercise, even if I was writing with no thought of publishing, and I abhor self-indulgence. You might as well know, before we go any further, that I was brought up rather badly, I think you would say, because the guiding principle was that one did not have any sort of entitlement in life, that no-one is much interested in what you feel, think or want. I cannot help it, I shall carry those ideas with me to the grave. For this reason, I find the modern obsession with 'self' puzzling and unhelpful. My experience of life, sad to report, has largely borne out my upbringing.

Enough of that. I mention it only to explain and excuse my reluctance to continue writing this book. Naturally, had I not written it you would not be reading it and would that have mattered? Hardly. So why did I pick it up again? Doing that actually made matters worse. I had started to be able to keep Lottie in a box marked don't go there, but then I came back to the book and she escaped. It has been a difficult experience, because life would have been easier if I had kept the lid on that box. Why I didn't, I'm not sure. No, I can offer no convincing explanation.

While I carried on writing the thought came to me to stop again, put it aside. I had plenty of other book projects on the go, so this was a distraction, but each time I did that I came back to it after a while. One of my fears has been that you might think it unrealistic that a person (dare I say it, a man?) could feel so strongly about a dog, and here I am going to accept that perhaps it is unrealistic.

As an aside, but not really, you may remember the death of Diana, Princess of Wales. I had no interest in the woman when she was alive, and even her death didn't mean a great deal to me, but as the whole business progressed, culminating in the orgy of her funeral, I shed tears like everyone else. I asked myself why, and I understood I wasn't crying for her at all, I was crying for everything and everyone I had lost, I was crying for loss itself. I was crying because Diana's funeral gave me permission to cry. I had, please remember, been brought up not to have feelings.

So this book is actually not entirely about my love for a dog called Lottie, it's about love itself. I have, and I offer this as just a fact, not a feeling, lived a life in which neither my parents nor my wives (2) had much love to give. I fully accept that may be down to me, but that is not the point (and here I have to admit to being a hopeless judge of character). The point is that in an unfriendly, even hostile, world, a dog came to my rescue and allowed me to give love, love that was absolutely unconditional. It is the love our dogs give us, and what Lottie also gave me, as well as her love, was someone to love.

I hope, therefore, that as you read this book you will get the point. If you are a dog lover yourself (and you probably are) you may take from it only those parts that inform you about a dog, a special dog as far as I am concerned, but still a dog. On the other hand, you might take rather more from it, and I won't know what it might be that you take, because that surely is up to you. Whatever you take, it is my hope, as with all my writing, that you enjoy what I have to say.

So, here's a question. Why did we, Liz and I, love Lottie? Well, first of all, doesn't everyone love their dog? I think we humans are hardwired to love animals, whether that's dogs or cats, or horses. I live on a farm, and many horses are kept here. The owners are all, to a man, women, but I have no idea why that would be. Now what surprises me is that they ride some of the horses but of course not all of the time. A horse (like a car I suppose), spends most of its life not being used (in this case, ridden), costing the owner a lot of money to stable and feed and care for, so what is that about? And some of the horses are never ridden. My favourite is a Welsh cob. She is lovely to look at, but she is not big enough for an adult to ride, so her owner is spending a great deal of money on what is effectively a pet, but which unlike a dog or cat does not live with her. She comes to the farm to visit, and I have to say keeping a pet that you visit is something I can't quite get my head round.

Anyway, my point about the horses is that they are

animals their owners love. Put another way, they serve the function of giving their owners someone to love. I know nothing of the lives of their owners, whether they have someone at home to love as well, but it does seem to me that what their horses are doing is to fulfil a role that no human can fulfil. Naturally, some of them have cats and dogs as well, understandably because they relate to domestic animals, but I see the love they have for their horses, something to be honest that had never occurred to me before I landed here after my marriage.

My point has been to look at the love humans have for animals other than other humans. It is very obviously something we need to do, and I am guessing it was instrumental in wolves attaching themselves to humans all those millennia ago. On this basis we were going to love Lottie come what may. I cannot guess, for myself, whether I would have loved her if she had been physically unattractive, because I'm afraid I am lookist. I'm not good at ugliness. Perhaps I just don't have a kind enough heart. But as it happens Lottie is very beautiful. Don't take my word for it. I have never yet met anyone who didn't ooh and aah when they saw her. I still carry her photo in my wallet, you know, the wallet where I'm supposed to keep photos of my grandchildren, and at any opportunity I whip it out to get people oohing and aahing all over again, and they always do.

1

The How and the Why

I hadn't wanted us to get a dog. Don't get me wrong, it wasn't because I don't like dogs, it was because I do like dogs. I love them. It was my wife I didn't love, and I knew, even though I didn't realise I knew at the time, that this wasn't going to last. Bringing a dog into our home (well, her home really, which I expect I shall come to) wasn't a good idea when there wasn't going to be a future. I was struggling to deal with a second failed marriage. A new relationship didn't make sense, and a dog would be a new relationship. If you're not a dog person perhaps you think a dog is simply a dog, but if you are a dog person you know a dog is a relationship. Of course, if you are not a dog person you probably won't be reading this, which you are so you probably are. On the other hand you might not be; you might have come to this by mistake, or perhaps you saw the title and thought a story of a man and his dog is a metaphor for something. I can't imagine what it could be a metaphor for, but what do I know?

Anyway, I was saying, about a new relationship. You might be thinking, this bloke is into dogs in a big way, perhaps he's not a people person, and you would be right.

No, I'm not going to give you a cliché about you can trust a dog but you can't trust people. I can't truly say what it's about. Dogs just make sense, people don't. And cats. You know where you are with dogs and cats. With people it's anyone's guess.

And this story starts with a cat. Actually two cats, Aggie and George. And I might as well introduce my wife at this point, because I shall have to sooner or later. I'll call her Liz. She said she was going to get a dog. You will notice that was she, not we. You don't want to know the details, but that will give you some idea that this wasn't a sharing kind of marriage. Aggie had died, and it hadn't been fair to bring a dog into the house with two cats but now we had one cat so we could apparently. Or she could.

So she asked me what kind of dog I like, and I said an Airedale Terrier. I like big dogs. It's a bloke thing, I think. A big dog is a real dog, a small one is, well, a toy. Cavemen didn't take a chihuahua hunting, they took something resembling a wolf. If you want something to keep your lap warm, get a cat is what I think. Or a hot water bottle.

Anyway, what kind of dog do I like wasn't a real question, it was an introduction to what kind of dog Liz likes. What she wanted was a dog small enough to pick up and take on a bus. Where this bus was going was never explained, but that was neither here nor there. A friend had recently died and left her £1000 to buy a dog (that was when you could get one for £1000), but apparently we weren't going to buy a pedigree dog, we were going to rescue one. Well, I had no problem with that, apart from a vague concern that rescued meant second hand, which is what happened and that, trust me, is going to be a big part of this story.

What came next was, I have to say, something of a surprise. We weren't going to rescue any old dog, we were going to rescue one from Romania. Huh? Were there not enough dogs in Britain looking for a home? The RSPCA must surely be crying out for homes.

Well, in fairness we did go along to the RSPCA, and the Dogs Trust, and neither of them had anything to suit, apparently. Liz is the only person I know who can stand in the entrance of a clothes shop, sweep her eye over the entire stock in ten seconds, and say, nope, they've got nothing I like. It might be a woman thing, or it might just be a Liz thing, but I have always found it a bit of a snap judgment. So anyway, no-one had a dog she liked so she did what you do nowadays, she went online. Well, I can tell you, do that and you will be spoilt for choice. It's like going into an orphanage with hundreds of children trying to catch your eye, pleading with you to take them home with you. Right now.

On the Web there are more dogs than you can shake a stick at; small ones, big ones, thin ones, fat ones, pretty ones, ugly ones (actually a lot of ugly ones), even three-legged ones. Liz is a soft touch (not for husbands, but you can't have everything, or in my case anything) and it was the ugly ones she felt for. Well, excuse me, I know I'm only the husband but no, I draw the line at ugly dogs. I know I said I love dogs, but by that I did not mean ugly dogs. And yes, I have to admire the plucky ones with three legs, and how much they get out of their three-legged lives is simply wonderful but they are not for me.

What we were looking for was a big dog that was small enough to take on this bus wherever it was going, long haired (for me), short haired (for Liz, who isn't heavily into vacuuming), with a full complement of limbs. In the end, of course, you get the dog you fall in love with (you also get the woman you fall in love with, which I think says everything about how stupid we men are).

Anyway, strangely we ended up with my perfect dog. Fully equipped on the leg side of things, big (well biggish), and wonder of wonders, long haired. And this is how it happened.

2

Lettie

The first thing we had to do was choose a dog from a selection of videos online, and Liz wanted to look at them all so that took a while but really, it was a bit pointless because we were just looking at videos of dogs, as a form of entertainment if you like, which is not the same thing as looking for the dog, you know, THE dog.

And there she was, a scrawny thing, black and tan, with a shaggy coat, but those are only physical characteristics. There was something else, don't ask me what, and we both felt it. This was our dog. Which was pretty surprising because the list of characteristics we had in our minds suddenly was irrelevant. She was our dog. Love at first sight. We had seen her for two minutes, and if we hadn't been able to have her we would have been bereft.

First, though, she had to have a cat test, which sounds like a CAT scan but is nothing like it. The people at the dog rescue kennels put her in a room with a cat to see if the dog would attack the cat. I don't know how many cats they lost doing the tests but I have a feeling it was something that seemed OK in Romania but would seem less OK here. However, we need not have worried. The cat wasn't fazed at all by the dog (perhaps it was a really laid-back moggie they used specially for these tests), but the dog was clearly afraid. A dog that was afraid of cats might seem strange but it suited us if we were going to bring her into George's home.

So that was that. Well, not quite, because we had to pay some hundreds of pounds for veterinary checks and rabies vaccination and pet passport and shipping, so it was I suppose a bit like adopting a Vietnamese baby except that it isn't and that's not something I've ever done so who am I to say?

It was our good fortune that the van driving all the way from Romania, across half of Europe, was arriving at Newhaven on the ferry and its first drop-off was in Brighton. We could only imagine how stressed a large van full of dogs was going to be after all that, and we were just pleased that ours was the first stop.

They carried her in and put her on the floor in our living room and then they were gone. No messing around, places to go, dogs to deliver. We peeked around the door of the living room, and there she was, shivering with fear, trying to push herself into a corner, clearly scared witless. If we hadn't loved her before we surely did now.

The paperwork said her name was Lettie, and the first thing we did was change that to Lottie, so that it was almost the same in case she was used to it, although I suppose that was unlikely as she had been living in a pound with hundreds of other dogs. Lottie sounded just a bit more recognisable than Lettie, anyway.

What had this animal been through, we could only try to imagine. Had she been scooped up from the streets of Targoviste by some brutal man whose job it was, who had no idea what that might feel like and would not have cared? Not knowing where you were, not understanding what was happening to you, not knowing what might happen to you next.

How long she was there for we couldn't know, but at some point she was scooped up and shoved harshly into a van, pulled out again, snarling in fear, and dumped into a cage with hundreds of other dogs, strange dogs she didn't know, howling in fear, or anger, or probably both. How much later we couldn't know, but at some point she was shoved into a room with a cat and she shouldn't have been but she was afraid of everything. Then back in the cage, perhaps fighting for food, maybe winning some fights or maybe losing them, who knows?

Then came the time she was dragged out and shoved into a van full of cages, each with a dog as scared as she was. Perhaps they were crying, perhaps they were silent, probably a bit of each. And then the long journey, days, across Romania, across Germany, then Belgium, cowering in the cage, getting out at stops for a few minutes of fresh air, then back in the hated van. What were those dogs thinking all that time, on the road, crossing the Channel in a van filled with the smell of frightened animals?

And then a stop, an open door, hands reaching in, and there she was, in a house where she couldn't recognise any smell, any sight. Was this filled with more fear for her, or was there at least some relief that the pervading smell of frightened dogs was absent? That the movement of the last couple of days had stopped? Well, of course we would never know, but she was now in our home, our life, and now we were inextricably part of her life and she was similarly part of ours. She didn't know it then, but she had landed on her feet, with people who already loved her, who were going to devote themselves to healing her scars and giving her the life they knew she deserved.

3

A Broken Dog

Where she had been put, on the floor of our living room, is where Lottie stayed. We peered through the window, and she was just lying there, shaking slightly, not looking round her, not interested, just staring at some fixed point. Was she in the room or was she in the van, or in the yard in Targoviste? How could she possibly comprehend what had happened to her, where she was, what these strange sights and smells meant? Did they mean danger? Dogs are intelligent animals. Her brain was surely trying to compute all of this. She must have been producing stress hormones, because why would she not be? We knew she was safe but she didn't.

We could never see her stand up. She just lay there. She ate the food we brought her once we left the room, and she used the toilet we cobbled together for her, but each time we came into the room she was curled up in the corner. We began to worry that she was paralysed, so we had to risk taking her to the vet to get that checked, knowing this was going to be another awful trial for her. She let the vet examine her uncomplainingly, and we were relieved to hear his verdict, that there was nothing structurally wrong with her legs. She was paralysed, but emotionally, not physically. We took her home, and perhaps, we couldn't know, going back to her room, with her own smells, was a little like coming home to a place she had started to feel safe. We didn't know but we wanted to think so.

This couldn't last for ever, and it didn't. The feeling of joy when we first saw her stand would be hard to exaggerate. I don't remember the first steps each of my children took, and I'm sure that was exciting, but in a very different way. I'm not going to compare children and dogs. The relationships are so different that would make no sense. The point for Lottie was that you know your children are going to walk but we couldn't be sure Lottie was going to stand, so this seemingly small thing was a sign, the very first one, that she might become a normal dog.

As it turned out, it was just that the journey this dog still had to go stretched out before her beyond any horizon she or we could imagine. And this small but big triumph tied her to us even more closely. We had seen this triumph, shared it with her, and so our emotional investment in her bound us together, though we didn't know it, forever.

Lottie was still a very broken dog, though. She displayed clear signs of being afraid of us. Dogs are hard-wired to connect with humans, and we suspected that somewhere in that dark place called her brain she was starting to look to us for the companionship that all dogs want. Could she be so very different? She was starting to accept that her food came from us, and regardless of the psychology her instinct for survival would surely mean that we were necessary for her welfare. She might still cringe when we came into the room, but we felt she was starting to compute that despite the fear, us coming in the room with food was a good thing. Dogs have been dependent on humans for thousands of years. They willingly made themselves dependent, and Lottie carried that genetic willingness. A part of her wanted to be our friend. All we had to do was teach her that she could trust us.

It was going to take baby steps. We, though, had made a commitment to her, even if we hadn't discussed it between ourselves. I think Liz and I saw things differently. Well, that was only to be expected. We saw pretty well everything differently. For what it's worth, here is an explanation that might help. Liz is strong on sympathy but weak on empathy. I'm the opposite. I can, I admit, be a little callous when I should be sympathetic, but I'm very strong on empathy. I can't go to a zoo, because I feel what the animals feel in their unnatural living conditions. Well, of course that's probably all nonsense. I doubt very much I can feel what an elephant feels. Not really. It just feels like I feel it.

And so I felt more closely connected to Lottie than Liz did. She felt sorry for her, but she lacked any mechanism for thinking like her. I looked into Lottie's soul and when I did that the fact that she was a dog and I was a man became irrelevant. This empathy was, I suppose, a good thing then, but a few years later, when I had to leave Lottie with Liz and go off on my own, it made it much, much harder than it might have been.

4

More Problems

Lottie's problems didn't stop with her mental health issues. She had physical problems too. From her mouth there hung an unsightly growth, and her flank was sore from a hotspot that she constantly worried at.

These were both problems that we could resolve, but one thing puzzled us. She had been 'sold' to us as a young dog, but her teeth clearly showed that could not be true. They were badly stained, as much brown as white, and we concluded from that that she must be a lot older than we had been told.

That, at least, turned out to have a simple answer. The vet knew immediately what it was about. Teeth discolouration is a sign a dog has had distemper. So Lottie had somehow come through that. In a big Romanian centre for stray dogs, where we knew animals were routinely put down to make room for more strays, someone had called a vet and that vet had treated what is often a lethal disease, all for a dog no-one wanted. We couldn't know why this had happened, but it definitely had.

And what this told us was that our Lottie had a strong and healthy constitution. She must have been malnourished, but she had fought distemper and won. Our dog was a fighter, and we felt pretty good about that.

She also had hard pads on her paws, and of course canine distemper is also known as hardpad disease. Her paws didn't bother her, until she was on a hard wooden floor and then she tended to slide a bit. But she could live a perfectly normal life with hard pads.

And before I come to her medical problems, there was something else we only learned about her once we saw her stand up. She only had half a tail. In the video we had seen online, she had a full tail, but she was also younger in that video, so between then and her journey to England she had lost half of it. What had happened? Had she been in a fight, had it got caught in something and had to be amputated? We were never going to know the answer to that, but it told us that she was indeed a survivor. Well, she had survived all sorts of horrors in her short life, and we were determined that she would from now on have the life she deserved. The life all dogs deserve. They depend on humans, so we have a responsibility to them. It was a responsibility that would test us with Lottie, but it was one we were never going to shirk.

And funnily enough, before long we couldn't imagine her with a full tail. In those early days what she had was permanently down, usually tucked between her back legs, but later, when she started to blossom, it spent much of its time sticking straight up, and as short as it was it became another part of her attraction.

Liz is good in a medical crisis. The nasty thing on Lottie's mouth didn't faze her, and as a homeopath she took Lottie to another vet, a homeopathic one, and the mouth thing had an easy resolution. The vet felt it was a reaction to the rabies vaccination, so he treated her for this and it cleared up pretty quickly. The hotspot, though, was a more intractable problem. She had a large bald area on her flank, and she constantly nibbled at it, which of course made it worse.

It took a long time to heal, but the vet was probably correct when he suggested it was a stress reaction. In a way it was healthy, which may seem odd, but her stress coming out on her skin was a lot better, for sure, than turning in on her, perhaps with a cancerous growth. As her stress level slowly reduced, and her nutrition improved, the hotspot gradually lessened and her fur started to grow back.

Liz put Lottie on a raw food diet, and we weaned her off the kibble she was used to. It wasn't a decision I was party to, but I did accept that on this she was right. I wasn't given a veto, but I didn't want one. Cats are fussy eaters but dogs are not. They eat to survive, and it takes something pretty unpleasant to put them off. Canine teeth are called canine teeth for a good reason. They equip dogs (and humans) to tear meat. Meat is a species-appropriate diet for dogs. I do sympathise with vegetarians who feed their dog a meat-free diet, and perhaps it can be done but I wouldn't do it. Cats, of course, are obligate carnivores, and not giving them meat would constitute abuse. In my humble opinion, if you are vegetarian, let alone vegan, and you can't bring yourself to feed meat to a cat, then just don't get one.

Which brings me to George. Lottie had been cat tested before she came to us, but George hadn't been dog tested. In the event we needn't have worried. Lottie wasn't going to bother him, and so he didn't bother her. George probably wondered about this dog in his house, but if he did he never mentioned it to us. His life continued much as before. He was getting on in years and he spent most of his day doing what cats are so good at, which is sleeping, mostly in the front garden, where people stopped to admire him and where he ignored people. Yes, come to think of it, George was good at ignoring, so that was what he did with Lottie, and if he didn't bother her she certainly wasn't going to bother him.

George had always been raw fed, so raw feeding Lottie wasn't difficult. She wasn't anything like as interested in food as most dogs (and she certainly wasn't as obsessed with food as a Labrador I know) and she was now being fed in the kitchen but she would only eat once we had left the room. In fact she much preferred to eat outside, so in all but bad weather we put her food out on the patio.

You might be wondering why we didn't feed her outside in the rain. After all, she was a working mountain breed. Rain, surely, couldn't bother her. Well, there I have to admit, as much as I love her, is a definite weakness in Lottie's personality. She hates rain. Actually, she doesn't like water anywhere. She will walk round a puddle that any normal dog would simply ignore. If she can't get round it she will step gingerly through it like a princess.

Apparently fear of water is a rabies symptom, so I agreed with Liz that Lottie's dislike of water probably stemmed from her rabies vaccination. She is a sensitive dog. In fact it was her sensitivity that almost cost her her life. More of that later.

And here's a princess and the pea story about Lottie. We knew she needed a small proportion of vegetables with her meat to give her a balanced diet, and she was all right with most veg, except peas, which she hated with a vengeance. We could mix all her food up, put one pea in it, mix it all up again, and when she finished there it would be, a single pea at the bottom of the bowl, as if she was thinking aha, they think they can fool me, but I'm cleverer than they are. Which may well have been true. Still, who hates peas that much?

5

A Phoenix called Lottie

Once she was back on her feet, both literally and metaphorically, we could start to work on Lottie's mental health. It was going to be a long road, and we were at the very beginning of it.

The first stage was to get her out in the garden. Apart from anything else, on a practical level the inside toilet, comprising layers of old sheets and blankets under a thick wad of newspaper, was putting a strain on the laundry. So after a few weeks I scooped her up in my arms and carried her outside. She shook violently but she let me do it. What she didn't let me do was put her down, She clung to me for dear life. She weighed twenty-three kilos, and her coat was more like a bear's than a dog's. Liz took a photo of her in my arms and yes, if you didn't know it couldn't be true you could have been forgiven for thinking she was some kind of bear. Anyway, that's by the by. This wasn't getting us anywhere, because standing in the garden with her was achieving nothing. Actually, what we didn't realise was that it was achieving something, because this was of course very new to her and she was taking it all in. Even the squawking of the seagulls, which we realised she had never seen before. Targoviste is not by the sea.

This went on for a few days, carrying her outside, bringing her back so she could use her inside toilet, until I took the bull by the horns and firmly put her down on the garden path. Upon which she scuttled away, keeping as low as she could, and hid under a bush. It's not easy dragging a 23 kilo bear dog out from under a bush, at least not without making her even more frightened, but it had to be done, because otherwise what was she going to do – stay there for ever?

After a few days of this it occurred to us that in fact it didn't have to be done, that leaving her under the bush wasn't such a bad idea. She couldn't get out of the garden, and from her hiding place she could survey the space around her, so suddenly it made sense. You learn from your mistakes. On my part I think I made those mistakes because I thought I was doing what she needed, but how could I know that?

All wild animals seek a safe space, and that is not in the open. Lottie was effectively a wild animal, and she was doing the obvious thing, making herself less vulnerable.

Now normally the way you train a dog is with food. They do something you want and you give them a treat and they learn what it is you want. Simple and effective. With Lottie, food was irrelevant. She had still not let us see her eating (she didn't know we peeked in at the window), so there was no way she was going to take a treat. A dog's natural instinct for food was there somewhere in her, but in those stressful moments when she was having to interact with us food became utterly meaningless. We thought a dog that had had to fend for itself on city streets would be more bribeable, but it showed just how stressed she was with us that she wasn't.

It was summer, and Liz and I spent time in the garden, with the living room window open so Lottie could hear us. From time to time we leaned through the open window and said hello, no pressure, just hello, and did we imagine it or was she getting used to us doing that?

Now we tried another little exercise. We were in the habit of sitting at the kitchen table last thing at night with a cup of tea, so we tried something pretty daring. We took our tea into the living room and sat on the floor with it, leaving her plenty of space to keep away from us. And miraculously that was what she did. It was miraculous because she got up and walked away. She had no idea what she had just done, but she had shown us that she could stand up and walk. It was enormous. OK, it might seem like it was for the wrong reason, but did that matter?

So each evening we settled on the floor, always with a treat on the floor just in case, and night after night there was no progress. It might seem to the reader that this would be dispiriting but it wasn't. We were in the same room, and even if she wasn't enjoying our company we were enjoying hers. And then, for some reason best known to herself, when we weren't especially looking she crept up and took the treat.

Looking back, at that point, it felt like we had come such a long way. We were under no illusion, there was still a very long way to go, but she was moving in the right direction. The thought that this was taking an inordinate amount of time, patience and energy never occurred to us even for a moment. This was what we wanted to do. It wasn't a chore, it was a pleasure.

No, I shall go further than that and say it was a gift. We were bringing this animal back from some dark place, with very little to go on but our instincts and our love, and she was rewarding us by coming back to life, slowly, erratically perhaps, but for certain. We knew by now that she was never going to be a normal dog. We hadn't bargained for this, so would we have taken her on if we had known? I doubt it. I can't speak for Liz, but an emotionally damaged dog, to me, is much the same as a three-legged dog. In fact it is much worse, because you are having to work on a part of the animal you can't see. In that sense, I suppose working with people with emotional problems is trickier than working with people with a physical ailment. You can't see the problem. We couldn't see Lottie's problems. On the other hand, they weren't that difficult to imagine.

6

The Garden

As we worked in the garden we called to Lottie. We reckoned she knew we were calling her, but it did occur to me that we might have to learn some Romanian, because would she understand English, but Liz was quite right when she said I was an idiot. It was, I claim now, a joke.

And then she did one of those things that regularly surprised us, on this occasion by putting her front paws on the windowsill and looking out at us. She was connecting, no doubt about it. I should have mentioned that in all this time we had never heard her bark. Just as we didn't know, when she came to us, if she could walk, we still didn't know at this point if she could bark. But she could, and she did. We both did a double take, not certain that we had heard it, but we had. She was talking to us. And hearing her voice made another connection with her. Now we could both see and hear her, and it opened for us another window into who she was.

She turned out to be a noisy dog, actually. Once she found her voice she used it rather more than Liz liked. I, on the other hand, never tired of hearing her.

Now she had found her voice, she regularly stood at the window and barked at us. We couldn't know what she was trying to say, but it was a reasonable guess that she wanted to be out there with us. In any case, that was what it looked like to us. She would get excited and bark and whinny, and her hard, sharp claws made marks on the windowsill that Liz wasn't happy about, but we both knew this was a stage she was going through, that sometime she would have the courage to come outside.

So the logical next step was to carry her out and walk her about on the lead, which was an improvement, because she no longer sought a hiding place but allowed herself to be gently led around. As soon as we took her off the lead, though, she headed straight for the door and in seconds she was back in the living room. Seconds later, she was up at the window again, so without wanting to push her too fast we gently led her out into the garden again. This way, she quickly learned that going into the garden wasn't dangerous, that she was free to go back to her safe place as soon as she was off the lead. Knowing this, it wasn't going to be too long before she no longer needed to.

It was frustrating, for us but also for her, when she barked at the window. We knew what she wanted and she did too, but she just couldn't bring herself to do it. We coaxed, we encouraged, we whispered sweet nothings, and she so wanted to believe us that it was safe but she was up against a blockage that she just could not find a way round. I would like to say we came up with some ingenious scheme to help her but it wouldn't be true. Perhaps none of what we did was very clever. It was always about showing her she was safe and then waiting for her to absorb that and believe it. That last bit she had to do on her own.

And finally the lure of the garden became stronger than her fear. One day we were at the far end by the garden shed and I nudged Liz and pointed my head, silently, in the direction of the back door. There she was, sniffing the air, hesitating but in some way willing herself to believe. And suddenly there she was, out on the path, smelling everything, on her guard for sure, but no longer scared. Well, perhaps a little.

We let her do her own thing, and she wandered, wandered note, not ran, back into the house. As with most things in her long slow development back to being a normal dog, each step took a long time but once it was taken there was no going back. Once she had stored some information it stayed with her. It was as if she enjoyed each new freedom and wanted to experiment with it, play with it if you like. It was just one of the things we noticed in her that convinced us of two things. The first was that she could be happy again, given time, love, patience and attention. Mind you, this assumes of course that she had ever been happy, and given her age when she was shoved into the dog pound in Targoviste it's probably not a safe assumption. In all probability she had never known happiness. Making Lottie happy had become an obsession with us, not only because we had fallen in love with her but because we had a duty to do that. The second thing we noticed was that she really was intelligent. Dogs are sometimes portrayed as dumb animals, and of course they can't do what we do, but in their own way they are truly intelligent. We judge them by our standards but that makes no sense. They have brains adapted to the life they lead, and they are often better at that than we are.

Humans are greedy and aggressive, obsessed with material things and prepared to hurt others and to trash the planet we live on to get what we want. OK, I fully accept that if dogs had developed to the point where they, rather than we, ruled the world, they might have turned out like us, but I am going to give them the benefit of the doubt and suggest they would simply have had more sense.

If you don't have a dog these things would never occur to you. Actually, even if you do they probably wouldn't.

7

Stairs

So far Lottie knew the ground floor of the house, and now the garden. She had never seen the other two floors. In fact, she could not even have known they existed. Had she seen us going up the stairs and wondered why? We thought not. Her home was the living room, and she spent very little time outside it. Even when she went out into the garden she was still coming back to go to the toilet. And we were still feeding her in the living room. In due course the entire house would be her space, but just now it was the one room.

So one day I picked her up, whispered gently in her ear that she should not be afraid, and slowly carried her up to the first floor landing. Slowly more for me than her. She was heavy. As soon as her feet touched the carpet she was off down the stairs. It was probably the first time in her life she had experienced stairs; we could tell that from the way she went down, carefully, not quite sure how they worked or why. Having reached the bottom landing she was back in her space, but instead of going into the living room she did something we could not have expected. She went back up the stairs. Then she ran down and then she ran up.

This dog learned fast.

She seemed to get some childlike pleasure from running up and down the stairs, and once she started we couldn't stop her, not that we wanted to. It was lovely to watch. Then we left all the doors open on the first floor landing and she explored each of the rooms. Liz and I both had offices on that floor, and we both had a sofa, and Lottie came to make both sofas her own. It came to be a great pleasure to work at my desk while she dozed contentedly three feet away from me. Sometimes I would just slide alongside her and stroke her gorgeous coat as she lay on her back and she would stretch her legs in pleasure, but that was later.

She slept on Liz's sofa too, when the fancy took her, but that turned out to be a bit of a problem. That room overlooked the street, and Lottie proved to be a very, very enthusiastic guard dog. She used the sofa to reach the windowsill, and she barked at every dog that went by. Her especial hatred was for a little three-legged dog we nicknamed Hopalong, on account of his being so happy with his condition, a condition I may have touched on before. Mind you, she hated all dogs. People she would tolerate, as long as they didn't wear a hoodie, and as long as they didn't stop outside the front garden for any reason. As far as Lottie was concerned, her territory extended to the pavement outside the house.

We soon learned, though, that she had a very particular venom for one type of visitor. Lottie hated foxes with a vengeance, and Brighton, like most towns I expect, has no shortage of urban foxes. They knew no fear, and soon learned to ignore Lottie as she barked furiously at the windows. Either that or they were teasing her. We couldn't leave her in that room during the night because at any time she was likely to start up and wake the neighbours. Closing the curtains was no help, because she could hear a fox through the double glazing and simply pushed the curtains aside. We were starting to get a reputation as noisy neighbours. There was obviously some genetic pre-disposition in Lottie's breeding that made her not only very protective but also really quite aggressive when needed.

Which led us to wonder about her breeding. It didn't take long, scanning the pictures of hundreds of dogs online, to see what she was. Up till then if anyone asked we simply said she was a Romanian Lert, on account of her being Romanian and alert, but now we wanted to know the truth.

There was one type of dog she seemed to conform to, and that was shepherd dogs, and narrowing it down we found one particular breed that was just like her in all but one characteristic. Lottie was clearly a cross-bred Carpathian Shepherd. She was a bit smaller and slimmer than the Carpathian, which is a pretty hefty breed, so we guessed her mum had been indiscreet with something like a German Shepherd.

It explained her aggression towards foxes. Carpathian Shepherds are bred to defend flocks of sheep from wolves, and even bears. As far as we could tell, they work in pairs and are left on guard overnight high up in the mountains of Romania. This also explained, a little later, why Lottie wanted to sleep out in the garden at night, something we really wanted to let her do but again couldn't because suburban Hove isn't the Carpathian Mountains. The neighbours really would have had something to complain about.

There was something else we were going to learn later. That being a shepherd dog very nearly cost Lottie her life. As I say, that was later.

8

Toilet Training and Other Things

Now it was time to get Lottie to use the garden instead of her indoors toilet. We were struggling to launder old sheets and blankets fast enough, and we were also struggling to collect enough old newspapers. And anyway, it was ridiculous, her going from the garden to the living room to do her business.

So, with some trepidation I have to say, we moved the toilet out onto the patio, in the hope she would recognise its smell and use it there. Or would she just go back in and do it on the rug? Something we had learned about Lottie was that it was nigh on impossible to guess what she was thinking.

She didn't use the toilet on the patio, but neither did she use the rug. For some reason that was not for us to know, she suddenly decided to be more dog and just go in the garden. You would have thought she had always done it, it came so naturally. Was she a fast learner, or had she been playing games with us, seeing how long we could keep up the indoor toilet thing? Were we anthropomorphising? Well, that was something we caught ourselves doing from time to time. As we tried to get into Lottie's head, we had to remind ourselves that she was a dog, not a small person. Liz did worry me a little, because she seemed to expect the dog to think like she herself would. As I think I've mentioned, Liz isn't good at empathising, and she had difficulty understanding that Lottie was not going to do logical human stuff. Not, dare I say it, that Liz herself often does logical human stuff.

Like toddlers who have accidents, Lottie had them. Sometimes we would find a wet patch on the first floor landing, and the other place she tended to go was on the carpet in Liz's consulting room, which made Liz very unhappy, and that was understandable. For some reason she never did it in my office. I like to think it was because she loved me more than Liz, but no, not really. I had had that carpet longer than I had had Liz, and I have it still. I suspect they will carry me out in it when my time comes.

I say Lottie had accidents, but thinking back perhaps she didn't. Was she doing it because she was stressed? I can't think why stress would make her do that, but then I'm not a dog. In any case she didn't do it often, and we kept a cleaning kit handy for emergencies.

Something she did which might well have been a stress reaction was chewing anything made of wood. We regularly found tooth marks on the wooden drawer handles of chests, the legs of chairs, even the base of the big pine dining table in the living room. One night, lying in bed up in our loft bedroom, where Lottie had not yet ventured, we heard a distinct chewing sound but decided to wait to investigate it in the morning. She was chewing the bottom step of the loft stairs. Now that was worrying.

The wood chewing wasn't a teething thing because she was too old to be teething. Did she need more fibre in her diet? I suppose it could have been boredom. Carpathian Shepherds are working dogs but she wasn't working, she was a house dog. Yes, perhaps it was boredom. There aren't many flocks of sheep in Hove, so there wasn't much we could do about that. In fact much later, when we took her for walks on the South Downs, she wasn't much interested in sheep, but then I guess why would she be? Her job was to protect them, not to chase them, in which case what she really needed was a wolf, but I have never seen one of those in Hove. Foxes, yes, but not wolves. Or bears, come to that.

And she sort of got over the wood chewing thing, but unlike normal dogs she never chewed sticks. If it hadn't been fashioned into furniture, wood just didn't interest her. Neither did she ever chase one if we threw it (stick, not chest of drawers). We bought balls, toys and all manner of things any normal dog would run after but we would throw whatever it was and Lottie would look at us as if to say, why did you throw that away, and wander off. She had no idea about that kind of play. She seemed to know she came from working stock and was determined not to take life frivolously.

Which wasn't completely true, because the one thing she liked to do was play tug. I had an old dressing gown which I put over me on the floor and she would pull at it for all she was worth. Maybe she saw me as a wolf. Anyway, it was great fun, except that she did have large teeth and she could hurt if I wasn't careful. Liz didn't do this with her, partly because she didn't want to get hurt but also, I suspect, because she doesn't have the same sense of fun. Anyway, you don't need to know that.

9

More Stairs and a New Bed

There was still more of the house Lottie hadn't seen. The top floor was our bedroom and bathroom. The stairs, though, were not carpeted, and Lottie had difficulty climbing them, with her long claws and hard pads, so the first time she ventured up she did so gingerly. She always had slight difficulty climbing them, and we could always hear her feet on the steps from anywhere in the house. Going down was a different problem for her. She would start carefully, then gather speed and sort of run down in a clatter.

So now she had the run of the entire house. For sleeping, she had her bed, which we put on the first floor landing, and two sofas, one in Liz's consulting room and one in my office. And in the course of time she starting sleeping on our bed. I had grown up with dogs and cats, and I like to have animals sleeping on my bed. Somewhere in our ancestry going back millennia we surely would have shared our sleeping arrangement with dogs, for warmth and protection. It seems very natural to me. Friends, mostly to be honest friends who were not dog people, were scathing about it, but that's their problem. I doubt very much that I shall ever live with a dog again, and that will always make me sad, but I shall always miss waking up in the morning to find a Carpathian Shepherd sleeping across my legs.

Liz wasn't so keen, and complained about the amount of space Lottie took and decided we needed a bigger bed. There were three of us in this marriage now and that required more space. Actually, there were going to be four but I shall come to that in due course.

And what a saga that was. It was a kind of Goldilocks story. The first bed was too something or other, the second one was too something else, and the third one was just right. It ended up costing £3000 to find the right king size bed that Liz could sleep in with me and the dog. What made things worse was that I knew this was all a waste of money because our marriage was going steadily downhill. I wished I could tell her not to spend the money because she wasn't going to need a king size bed much longer, but there is a right time for everything and this wasn't it. Funnily enough, after I left Lottie slept with her even more and she came to like it. Maybe the problem all along had not been Lottie but me.

10

Venturing Out

By now Lottie was going for short walks, very short walks, on the lead, up and down the alley by the house. Liz is a morning person, and each day before it was quite light she walked the dog up and down the alley, stopping where it came out onto the street because Lottie would not go any further. She stood at the exit and looked wistfully (Lottie, not Liz), but nothing would persuade her to venture any further.

Liz decided it was time to seek help from an expert dog behaviourist. His name was Brian, and he came highly recommended. He would understand Lottie, she felt sure. Except that he didn't. He sort of knew his stuff, but it was all theory. When it came to actually engaging with Lottie he was no better than we were. Was it dogs in general, in which case how had he come recommended, or our dog in particular? In fairness to him, Lottie is not normal, and I just don't think he had the expertise to handle a problem dog. I expect he knew what to do with aggressive dogs, which was probably a type he often had to help with, but Lottie was not aggressive, she was afraid. True, aggression in a dog can be the result of fear, but it was not how

Lottie's fear manifested itself. Anyway, the long and short of it was that Brian, like the first king size bed, had to go. In this case I had to agree with Liz's decision. Well, I had to agree with all her decisions, but what I mean is I did so of my own volition.

The next behaviourist was Mike. He really did know his stuff, and he was instrumental in Lottie's development. He was a very annoying person, and he and I fell out, but I have to give credit where it's due. He did something pretty miraculous.

He asked us what single thing we wanted Lottie to be able to do. We (when I say we this should be taken to read Liz) said it was walking on the pavement. Venturing beyond her safe space, even walking as far as the recreation ground just a few doors down. OK, he said, let's do that. And we did. Don't ask me how. To this day I can still only believe he somehow took control of Lottie in a way we had never been able to do. Actually, now I think about it, I suspect I do know the answer, but I shall come to that shortly.

We set off, and she followed on the training lead, hesitantly, but she did follow. From time to time she sat down and said she wasn't going any further, in that way dogs communicate, and Mike said we should let the lead go slack, but only for a few seconds to let her settle down, and then gently pull to tell her we were in charge, not her. Now I knew what Liz had been doing with me all these years, albeit not visibly with a lead.

We got to the rec and in we went, and we carried on walking, and then we took her home, and Lottie in some way we didn't understand had made a giant leap forward. And as with everything she achieved, once she had done it she found it easy to keep doing it, as if she had always done it and didn't know what the problem was. Lottie's brain seemed to have a series of doors; they stayed shut until you somehow made them open, and then they stayed open. I'm only an amateur psychologist, but perhaps that's not so different from humans. Once we learn something we don't normally unlearn it. On reflection perhaps that's what we call progress. There is a downside for us humans, I think, in that we are unable to see that progress isn't always progress. Once, for example, we have invented nuclear weapons, we can't uninvent them. Once we have created technology that we know is trashing the planet, we just keep creating more. When we find ourselves in a hole we just keep digging. How lucky the other animals are not to have that flaw in their personalities.

What wonderfully simple lives they lead. All a dog or a cat wants is regular feeding, a place to sleep, some human company (that's more dogs than cats) and although they don't know it the only other thing they need is for every day to be the same as every other day. We are just the opposite. We're restless, and we want every day to bring something new. Who, I wonder, is happier? Watching Lottie and George, I did sometimes envy them their simple contentment.

So here is the answer I just said I would explain. It was to do with the bust-up between Mike and me. He complained that when I had Lottie on the lead I wasn't following his instructions. I replied that I was quite happy to do that, but being a grown-up human I did want to know why, what he was thinking. In short, I wanted to know what he knew about Lottie, who was after all our dog not his. His response came as something as a shock. He said it wasn't for me to question his instructions but to follow them. Now leave aside for a moment that we were a paying customer and that's not really good customer relations, it didn't in any case make sense. How were we going to learn unless he explained himself? The point was though that it made perfect sense to him. He was the leader of the pack. In his strange world, I was just another dog, and I was expected to follow the leader, not argue with him.

I know, barely believable, but I promise you it was true. And it explained what he had done with Lottie. His entire being was predicated on being the leader of the pack. Lottie had seen that and responded to it the only way she could, the way he knew she would, by following. All we had to do after Mike was to get her to transfer her allegiance from him to us, which surprisingly we did.

Mind you, Liz carried on working with Mike for a while after that. He said to my face that he wouldn't work with me, in my own living room (well, Liz's living room), so I left the room and never saw him again. I got regular reports as to what a wonderful job he was doing with Lottie, but I could see the change in her so I didn't really need the reports. Or maybe it was just Liz's way of saying he was right and I was wrong.

42

11

A Progress Report

I would say there were four elements to the progress we had made with Lottie up till now, four things we did that I'm not saying she wouldn't have got elsewhere but that she was fortunate to get with us all the same.

The first was our undivided attention. We were fortunate to both work from home. Liz had recently retired from her day job and was practising as a homeopath, and I'm an author so obviously I work from home. It meant we were able to be there for Lottie, stop doing what we were doing whenever there was something we could usefully do for her. Was this a chore? No, not at all. We should not have done it if we hadn't been committed from the very beginning. People said she was lucky to have us but we turned that on its head. We felt lucky to have her. We had both brought up our separate families years before and I venture to say that we are neither of us natural parents. We didn't have a lot in common but this one thing we did, a natural instinct to devote ourselves to this dog. Is that excessive, perhaps a bit eccentric? Not for me to say. Probably. OK, yes, it is, but come on, why not? We are what we are, etc.

The second element came from the first. We devoted this much time and attention to Lottie because we were genuinely interested in how she functioned. It was, if you like, an experiment or intellectual exercise, not that either of us was ever going to write a scientific paper about it, although funnily enough one of us did in the end decide to write a book about it, which you have probably noticed. I must add that this book was never planned. Lottie is now five years old and it's two years since I have seen her. I had recently finished another book in my field of healthcare, and I don't know how to get up in the morning and not write. I could have turned to my fiction writing but suddenly I couldn't get Lottie out of my head or my heart, and here we are.

Anyway, back to what I was saying about the amount of intellectual work we put into learning how to help Lottie. She has had four trainers / behaviourists in her life with us, she has cost more than we would have spent on a pedigree pup, but as I write this, for the first time I think I really appreciate how much she has taught us. Back to her though, and I believe I can state that one reason for her success has been the sheer amount of work we have put into developing her.

The third element has been her diet. It hasn't always been easy. While Liz and I were together I was responsible for most of her feeding. We bought pork steaks and chops, lambs liver and kidneys, turkey joints, beef skirt and chicken. Raw bones were an important part of her diet from the beginning, but because her teeth had been weakened by the distemper she couldn't chew some of the big bones a dog of her size would normally have. And one of her annoying habits has always been to pick up a bone and take it upstairs to chew. Greasy marks on the carpets were just part of the cost of letting this dog do what she needed to do. You might be thinking at this point that we indulged her too much, that she lacked discipline. We didn't and she didn't, but there would have been no point disciplining her to fit in with our lifestyle simply because that was our lifestyle, like it or not. Here perhaps you might think we were being indulgent, but I think keeping a dog is a compromise. A dog is a domesticated wild animal (so is a cat, with more emphasis on wild and less on domesticated), and I believe it behoves us to respect that. Dogs voluntarily became domesticated long ago, but if we don't understand their genetic heritage I think we fail to give them what they need but we also compromise the relationship that both parties should benefit from. Dogs need discipline, because they are pack animals and the pack has a leader and followers, and for sure humans in this relationship have to accept the role of leader or chaos follows, but any leader who fails to understand their followers is destined to be disappointed.

The final piece in the jigsaw is veterinary medicine. Lottie has always been under-medicated, under-vaccinated and has seen both allopathic and homeopathic vets, according to her needs. It was an allopathic vet who almost killed her, which I have already mentioned, but I promise I shall get to that in due course. In medical terms, pets suffer from the same problem as humans. People eat rubbish, drink and smoke and take recreational drugs, and then they expect a doctor to make them better. Many pet owners feed their animals badly on mass-produced pet food with no idea about what has gone into it. Vets will tell you that many cats and dogs are overweight, because they are overindulged – overfed on rubbish and under-exercised. Just like people.

Lottie has always been fed well, on a species-appropriate diet, and she gets a walk on the South Downs every day (as long as it's not raining when she pokes her nose out of the door!). I'm guessing that shepherd dogs, unlike sheepdogs, are bred to save their energy. A dog protecting flocks in hill country isn't going to use its energy herding the sheep, and it certainly isn't going to run around madly like some mutt chasing a ball in a park, it is going to sit and watch, conserving its energy to survive in harsh conditions and remain alert for threats. That was exactly what Lottie did. The longer she was with us, the more we saw her genetic inheritance come out. And the more improvement there was in her health, both physical and mental, the closer she got to the dog she was supposed to be. Having said that, it was fortunate, at our age, that she didn't need constant exercising.

So that's where we were up to after about a year. Now here's some more about what happened next.

12

Something We Weren't Expecting

When we got Lottie we were assured she had been spayed, but we realised this wasn't true when she came into season. And what you might think should be a simple matter turned out not to be simple at all.

We put off doing the spay after her first season, because she found visits to the vet so stressful. In any case, that and her second season were not very marked, so we always had some doubts. Perhaps she was having some kind of pseudo or phantom season. Perhaps she had been spayed after all. We were told the local dog dogs would detect her being a bitch on heat and bother her when we took her out, but that didn't happen. So perhaps she wasn't really on heat. Either that or she just wasn't attractive, but I chose not to believe that. Lottie is beautiful. How could any dog resist her? Well, I suspect the answer to that was that almost all the dogs we came across were not intact males. They had been done. They wouldn't have known what to do with our bitch if she had taken them behind the bushes for a quickie. Not that she would have done such a thing.

There were in the end two compelling reasons to have

her spayed, come what may. One was the health risk to her of not being done. We were warned in no uncertain terms of the risk of pyometra, which was likely be fatal. The other was that Lottie was prone to skin problems, and when she came into season this got much worse and she itched terribly. It caused her, and us, considerable distress.

So we bit the bullet and took her for her operation. The nurse administered a pre-med while she was with us, and then as Lottie became drowsy she manfully picked her up and carried her into the operating room. I wanted to go with her but wasn't allowed as the room was sterile. We were advised to go home and wait for them to call us to pick her up.

Well, they did call us to pick her up, but it wasn't what we were expecting. It was in fact much too soon. They had not done the operation, because Lottie had had a major reaction to the anaesthetic. Major turned out to be a euphemism for life threatening. She was unconscious when we collected her, and remained unconscious for some time after we got her home. Liz rang the homeopathic vet and was given advice about a remedy to counteract the drug, and this brought Lottie round. There was no serious danger by now, but we were in shock.

Once we calmed down and it became clear she wasn't any longer in danger, we had time to ask ourselves a question. Why had the veterinary practice asked us to take her home? Surely they should have kept her for observation, until she came round. Surely you don't put a dog in danger and then push her out of the door. It's something we have never been able to find a satisfactory answer to. I didn't say anything to Liz, but the thought occurred to me that they wanted her out of the door because if she died in our care they were going to less liable than if she died on their premises. Just saying.

That was when we learned that there are certain anaesthetic drugs that cannot be given to shepherd dogs. Either the vet had not know that (when of course he should) or he hadn't recognised Lottie's breed (which he also should). Anyway, she survived and we were grateful for that.

Once we recovered from this we were left with the fact that Lottie was still at risk from not being spayed, but it wasn't something we could begin to contemplate for her, though it wasn't something we could simply ignore for ever either. Well, we ignored it for a while. Then Liz had the very sensible idea of a laparascopic spay, which would be minimally invasive and thus require far less anaesthesia. Could she find a vet to do that? Not for a hundred miles, which would have meant transporting Lottie both before but especially after the operation, neither of which was desirable. So it was back to the drawing board.

And in the end we simply had to bite the bullet again, but this time with a vet who assured us he knew what anaesthetic drug a shepherd dog can and can't have. You can imagine, even so, how worried we were. I took her, on my own this time, and pulled up outside the practice, and that was as far as we got. Lottie would not get out of the car. She knew, and nothing I said could stop her knowing. The only way this could be resolved was with brute force, and I wasn't going to do that. She was stressed enough already. So it was Lottie one, vet nil. I worried I was going to be in trouble with Liz about this but in the event she

49

was, I thought, quite glad it had happened.

Still, once again we were back where we started. Some time passed, and then some more time passed, and no amount of ignoring it was making the problem go away. Then suddenly, it did just that. We found a vet who ticked all the right boxes, and before we could change our minds she was whisked in and it was done. I know, you're thinking come on, it's just a dog and it's just an operation a million dogs have had before, and we kept telling ourselves that. Well, the second part, not the first one. Neither of us had had a child needing surgery, but I expect that would have been almost as bad.

We collected her from the practice and there she was, absolutely fine, albeit with a big bald patch where her girly bits had been removed (I'm not hot on the female anatomy), and the nurse was putting one of those collars on her, you know, the ones that stop the dog nibbling the scar. Well, I could have told her that was not going to work, and in fact I did tell her. I couldn't speak for other dogs, but there was no way ours was going to cope with that. I mean, quite apart from anything else how does a dog sleep with that thing round its neck? We asked if there was an alternative, and surprisingly there was, in the form of a bright red stretch suit that went round her and press studded underneath. I thought she wasn't going to like this but it was infinitely better than the collar, and in any case she didn't seem to mind it as it happened. We had to undo it behind her bottom when she went out into the garden, for reasons I don't need to explain, and apart from that she was fine.

Well, we had passed another milestone. I mean she had

passed another milestone. Well, all right, we had passed it together.

13

Lulu

George was old by now, and his health was deteriorating before our eyes. I think most pet owners have had to make that decision – when do you stop keeping them alive when it is clearly their time to die? You tell yourself it's for them, that they haven't given up yet, but more often than not it's not for them it's for you. How we would cope if it ever becomes legal to euthenise the incurable sick, I don't know. Would it be easier to have my grandmother put down than George? Well, since I haven't got a grandmother that's a question I will never have to answer. We took him into the vet's consulting room, and he lay there, not knowing what was going to happen, and probably he wouldn't have cared if he had known. It was his time. I just hope someone does me the same kindness one day.

In the event, though, I chickened out. I suddenly could not get it out of my head that he had trusted us each time we had taken him to the vet and now we had tricked him. I know, it's nonsense, but I can only tell it like it was. I left Liz to deal with it. She's better in a crisis than I am. Perhaps, and it may be unkind to mention it in this context, she could do it because she doesn't empathise, and I couldn't do it because I do.

We buried him in the front garden under the very patch of grass where summer after summer he had loved to sleep in the sun. It's sentimental nonsense, I know, but it's what we did.

Liz said since we have a dog now we wouldn't have any more cats. In any case, she was fed up with them killing the local wildlife. Aggie had been a birder, and George's favourite prey was the frogs from the pond. Sometimes they died, from fright possibly, but more often than not we got them away from him and put them back in the water. We knew he was going to fish them out again, and I don't know but perhaps they did too. Perhaps they got used to it. On reflection, probably not.

So, no more cats. Until one day, not a few months later, that decision was rescinded and we were going to get another cat after all. The wildlife killing thing, it seemed, no longer mattered. Oh well, it was all the same to me. Lottie was enough for me, but a cat, well, that would be good too.

For Lottie's sake it would need to be a kitten, or at least a young cat, one that would accept her dominance in the house from the beginning. So it was back to the RSPCA, on the off chance that they would have a kitten, and blow me but they did. I had hoped for ginger. For some reason I have always wanted a ginger cat but never had, and I wasn't going to get one again. Liz had always had black and white cats. She's a black and white sort of person. She doesn't do shades of grey.

And what colour was this serendipitous kitten? Yes, black and white. Still, she was, it has to be said, incredibly cute. Well, of course she was cute. Have you ever seen a kitten that isn't? Unfortunately, though, just as we came to look at her so did another family. They were undecided, and I sent them evil thoughts to help them do so, and it worked. They didn't want Pearl (strangely, the name the staff had given her), because she was lame. Well, a lame cat! Could one ask for more? I put my hand in her cage and she held on to it as if to say yes, I choose you; I was smitten with the kitten and there was no turning back.

Well, of course you have to prove you are suitable adopters and have no connection with the Russian mafia or whatever it is these people look into, and we passed all the tests, including the one where two RSPCA ladies came to the house to make sure it was good enough for a stray cat, which notwithstanding Lottie's insane barking it was. And suddenly we were a family again. The first thing we had to do was change this kitten's name. I mean, who has ever heard of a cat called Pearl? No, it was horrible; that was something we both agreed on. So she got changed to Lulu, which was something I agreed on. I didn't really care what she was called. Well, as long as it wasn't Pearl.

She was restricted to the living room to start with, which was funny because that was where Lottie had started. To say she settled in instantly would be an understatement. Despite her limp she tore around the room chasing anything that could be chased, and we fell in love with her. Well all right, I did. Liz said she did but actually she has never really loved Lulu. Don't ask me what that's about. She had loved all her other cats but this one she didn't connect with. Not that Lulu minded. I mean, she's a cat.

They don't have to be loved the way dogs do.

And talking of dogs, how did Lottie take to this bundle of playfulness? Well, I think the best way I can describe it is to say she didn't care. Lulu simply meant nothing to her. Actually, that's not exactly true because she was a little afraid of her. Yes, Lottie was more scared of Lulu than Lulu was of her, despite their enormous difference in size. It's a cat and dog thing. If you've got both you will probably know that cats don't stand for any nonsense from dogs in the house, and dogs learn to fear them. I did say that both dogs and cats are domesticated wild animals; well, Lulu had some genetic inheritance which enabled her to bully an animal many times her size.

It took a couple of years but they did come to some sort of understanding, and I knew they were going to be all right when one day Lulu jumped up onto the sofa in my office where Lottie was sleeping, and curled up herself. Fair enough they were tail to tail, but from that day they did it regularly. It was usually Lottie first, but if Lulu was on there Lottie would sometimes creep up carefully and curl up at the other end to ensure they kept a respectful distance.

Lottie was fed on the kitchen floor unless she was eating outside, so because they were eating the same meat we put Lulu's dish on the kitchen windowsill. She wasn't a big eater, and Lottie learned to sit and look at the windowsill in hope, and we got into the foolish habit of putting the dish on the floor for her to finish. Foolish because cats like to graze. Half an hour later Lulu would come back for more and wonder why her plate was empty. She got her own back though. When we gave Lottie bones she would usually leave them for later, but Lulu didn't waste any time. She would drag a bone out of the dish and chew on it for ages. We told Lottie Lulu would do this if she didn't hurry up and eat them, but that was a lesson she never learned. I suspect our cat has some dog genes in her.

14

First Steps

This story is not told in chronological order, partly because things didn't happen like that and I need to divert to things that happened connected with other things I'm telling you about, if that makes sense, but also because I have to admit my memory of the chronology is hazy. I can remember what happened but I'm not so good on when it happened, so I hope you will forgive me if this doesn't always make complete sense, if sometimes you have to say, hold on, when did that happen? Anyway, does it matter?

The biggest single challenge we faced was getting Lottie to overcome her fear. She was afraid of other dogs, and people, and the outdoors. The problem with that was that the outdoors is full of people and dogs, so it kind of all came together in one big horrible problem. Well, obviously our strategy was to tackle the outdoors thing where there were unlikely to be people or dogs. It was a very sensible strategy, albeit a difficult one to actually carry out. Where do you go? To a park? No, people and dogs are a park kind of thing. On the Downs? Well, the Downs are big, and that was where we started, staying in the car until we were quite sure we were alone.

(Here is a by the way. My car was not ideal for carrying Lottie, because it had leather seats, and as much as I loved her I loved my car too. When there was no choice, I put a blanket on them but she tended to slide around on that so it wasn't a great solution. So we always used Liz's car as much as possible. That had the added advantage of being a hatchback, and although the hatchback bit wasn't big enough for Lottie so she went on the back seat, it came into its own when we parked and could open the back for her to sniff the outdoors.)

She was quite interested to look out of the back window at the world, but she had no intention of taking that any further. Inside the car was a safe space, outside was not. If we did try to hold her and coax her out, albeit gently, she would just shuffle over to the other end of the seat, so we soon accepted that was not going to work. What all this meant was that for a long time all we did was take her for a ride, stop somewhere for her to look out, and drive home. As far as it went, you might say if was progress of a kind, but it wasn't a lot of that. Looking back, we may have been underestimating its value, because even though she doggedly refused to get out of the car, the more she sat and looked I think the more her brain started to work out that outside the car might not be such a terrible place. So we had to keep taking her for rides while she figured it out. Did we ever force the issue and pull her out? No we did not. Looking at the fear in her eyes, the only possible effect of forcing her would have been to increase that fear. This was something she was either going to do or not do, but if she did it it was going to be in her own time, when she was ready. You might think we had enormous patience, and there you would be right. Liz wasn't always patient, whereas I am patience personified. I can wait for ever. I am still waiting, at the age of 70, to decide what I want to be when I grow up.

The day we finally got her out of the car is vividly recorded in my memory. It was in a small car park on the Downs. Actually, I say I remember it but I can't actually recall why she got out, even though I do remember what happened next. I wish I could remember why she did it, because that surely would be really significant, I mean to understand what the process was in her brain. I can only say that it was just something whose time had come, like going up the stairs at home. Maybe it was some smell she picked up that we didn't. We shall never know, and anyway does it really matter?

In fact whether Lottie sniffed the ground was always a big issue, because sniffing became a sign that she was relaxed, enough anyway to be more dog. As she developed into a more normal dog, I should say that Lottie sniffed rather more than I see other dogs doing. I know they pick up information about other dogs from the scent they leave behind, and that was one aspect of normality that became really quite important to her. One of my memories of Lottie is that her nose rarely left the ground. I expect it had something to do with her breeding.

Anyway, on the day in question she didn't sniff. That would come later. She dragged me round at the other end of her lead, and then she headed back for the car. When I say she headed back, I'm talking about a very short distance, nothing so brave as letting the car out of her sight.

(And here's another by the way. Liz's car back then was purple, it's a Brighton thing, which you might think would make it easy to identify in a car park. I don't know if dogs recognise colours, but Lottie certainly didn't. At the end of a walk she would just stand by the first car she came to, and when we didn't open it up she went and stood by the next one.)

Because this particular spot was where she had braved the outside world, we made it the place we took her to every day, so she could become familiar with it and feel safe. More often than not she just went round in a circle for a few minutes and then headed back to the car, but this new Lottie, compared to the old Lottie, was such a revelation we could only see it as progress.

The next stage was that she let us lead her along the path that ran away from the car park. She was reasonably happy with this, but she would suddenly stop and turn back for the car, with such a sense of urgency it would surely have been unthinkable not to let her even if we could have stopped her.

It was on one of these short walks that she first became acquainted with cows. Well, when I say acquainted, I do mean from a distance, and always from the other side of a fence. Did she see them as overgrown dogs? Either way, she did not like them. They were mildly curious about her but since she gave them a wide berth, especially when crossing a cow field on a public footpath, they soon lost interest. Just occasionally one would follow her, but even if she wasn't a fast runner she was a faster runner than a cow!

Cows are strange animals, placid looking yet really

unpleasantly menacing when they take an unwanted interest in you. They can of course be very dangerous, but there are simple rules when walking dogs in cow fields, and the most obvious one seems to me to be avoid eye contact at all times. Whistling a happy tune also seems to help, because even if the cows don't know what it means you know it means you are pretending you're not scared. My policy is always to accept that this is private property we are allowed to cross by law, but private all the same, that cows are valuable beasts, and that it is my responsibility, not the farmer's, not to cause trouble. Anyway, since Lottie was more scared of them than they were of her we never had any trouble.

I did wonder how she would respond to sheep, and in some parts where we walked her there were unfenced sheep, but if she had any sheep-related genes in her they never showed themselves. Sheep, of course, will always run away, and what is important to remember is that a farmer who has had a bad experience with dogs will feel perfectly entitled to shoot first and ask questions later. That Lottie was never going to hurt his flock would have been one of those asking later questions. In any case, Carpathian Shepherds are sheep protectors, not herding dogs like, say, Collies, and that was probably why it never occurred to Lottie to chase them, herd them or do anything else with sheep.

15

Walkies

Lulu really was part dog. I had got into the habit of taking Lottie to the recreation ground late in the evening for a last walk. She loved the darkness and was always more relaxed then. And little Lulu got into the habit of coming for a walk with us. She trotted along (well, more limped, actually), sometimes in front, sometimes behind, and from time to time she would leap out and bop Lottie on the nose. That, I can tell you, did not go down well. As much as Lulu tried to get Lottie to join in the fun Lottie simply ignored her. Lulu, in her opinion, might think she was a dog but that was a misunderstanding on her part.

There were two things about the rec that Lottie liked. One was the children's playground area, where the sign on the gate said No Dogs but Lottie couldn't read English so that didn't matter, and the other was foxes.

Foxes loom large in Lottie's life. Whether that is because she hates them or because she sees them as animals to play with I couldn't say. She has never caught one, on account of them being able to run faster than her, and what she would do if she ever got one cornered I dread to think but luckily she never has. They seemed to think she was an animal to play with, because they would come out from behind the bushes and sit there looking at her, seemingly daring her to give chase, which she always did. It's something to do with the night, because the foxes come out at night and Lottie hunts at night, but how serious any of it is I have no idea.

Incidentally, it was strange but when I shone the torch across the field and picked up the reflection in a fox's eyes, like cats eyes in the road, my brain found it easy to compute that it was a fox but Lottie never could do that. I guess I was computing what the torch was doing but a dog knows nothing about man-made technology so it cannot know what a pair of glinting eyes signifies.

Lottie was really determined about foxes. I always put her on the long lead when we were leaving the rec to go home, and one evening I had just clipped her on when she spotted one and gave chase. I was forced to let go of the lead to avoid damage to my hand, the fox disappeared into the bushes and Lottie followed. What I didn't know was that fox and dog had shot through a hole in the chain link fence into the nursery beyond. I called and whistled, but Lottie has pretty well no recall so why I bothered I don't know but it's just something you do even when you know it's pointless. A bit like life in general, I should say, doing stuff you know is pointless, in the forlorn hope that what has never worked before will suddenly change its mind.

Anyway, on this occasion, as expected she didn't come back. So in the dark I got down on hands and knees and crept through the bush and then through the hole in the chain link fence, and there she was sitting quite still, making no sound, just waiting for me to rescue her. The five-metre lead was wrapped round a tree and she was incapable of moving. Any normal dog would bark to say here I am but Lottie, as I think I have mentioned before, is not normal.

So I unwrapped her from the tree and led her back, on my hands and knees, through the hole in the chain link fence and through the bush, and when I stood up in the lamplight I saw what I had not noticed, which was that the ragged edge of the chain link fence had done what ragged edges do, it had ripped my perfectly good trousers to shreds.

You love your children no matter what they do, even if sometimes you wish they didn't. Did I say children? I mean dog.

16

Bedtime

Lottie wasn't keen on dog treats but somehow we got into the habit of giving her one of those dental sticks that are supposed to help clean their teeth. Whether they do or not I don't know, and I suspect they are full of rubbish, but her diet was good enough that a little junk food wasn't going to much matter. She knew, when we came in from the rec, that I would go to the cupboard and get one out for her.

And as much as she loved this treat, it was a reminder of her troubled brain that sometimes she would not come and get it. She wanted it. We knew that and she knew it, but she couldn't bring herself to come and take it from me. I could see, watching her sit there a few metres away, that there was some battle going on in her head, do I or don't I? It was impossible to imagine what her problem was, because she loved me and trusted me, and she loved the treat, but still something, somewhere in the recesses of her damaged mind, something said don't. It was a sad reminder that she might appear normal most of the time but she wasn't.

When she did take the stick she would always run happily upstairs to chew it, and that, as simple as it was, was a great pleasure to me. Those few seconds of happiness over something so small was for some reason a joy to watch. Strangely, she would never take it out into the garden. Even if I gave it to her there, or at the back door, she would then run upstairs with it. This was part of a syndrome that a vet was later to put a name to, but it didn't matter. If she was happy we were happy.

She had a choice of beds to sleep in. There was ours, with us, there were two sofas (not including the good one in the living room which she wasn't allowed on) and her dog bed, which sometimes we put on the first floor landing and sometimes in our bedroom, always trying to guess what she wanted. And of course if none of these was good enough as a last resort there was always the floor, anywhere.

I have to confess here that if she came into the bedroom I encouraged her to jump up onto the bed. Sometimes she would and sometimes she wouldn't, and when she did she didn't usually stay for long. Lulu also liked sleeping with us, which Lottie wasn't keen on but she put up with it. The cat in any case preferred to sleep under the duvet, which Lottie wasn't allowed to do, and her favourite place was curled up next to me. That was fine, except when I turned over Lulu then had to come out from under the duvet, walk round my head and back under so she could sleep at my front again. As much as I like sleeping with animals, that did get slightly tiresome. You will not be surprised, though, that whatever Lulu wanted Lulu got. Whether that's because she was strong willed or I was weak willed I don't know. Probably a bit of each. I was sleeping with three females and I knew when I was beaten.

When I was growing up we had five Siamese cats, and mine, Tikki, slept spread across my neck, after she had first thoroughly washed my ears. Lulu thankfully did neither of these things.

Lottie didn't in any case sleep with us for long. She would get up and prowl round the house. She is an excellent guard dog, always ready even when asleep to detect any threat. Anyone foolish enough to try it on with her would regret it. She's only the size, say, of a smallish German Shepherd, but you would not want to get on the wrong side of her. Dogs, as I have already said, are domesticated wild animals, and some of them, like Lottie, have been bred for a particular purpose, and to be honest you should never take liberties with any dog, even the little fluffy ones. It's a lesson children have to learn, and if parents don't teach them to treat all dogs with respect, not just dogs they don't know but their own pets, they are being remiss.

It's something Liz always worried about, that Lottie would turn on some child out on a walk. She never did, but she fantasised about the worst possible scenario, ending with Lottie being put down because some parent complained that she was vicious. Well, as I say, all dogs have the potential to be vicious and it was a long time before we would trust Lottie to behave, off lead, when there were children around. With all that stuff going on in her head, could we ever completely trust her?

Interestingly, although she chased cats in the rec she

never chased Lulu, so I guess she had accepted this new cat as one of the family. It was a huge pleasure to see the two of them sleeping together, for me anyway. Lulu also got some kind of pleasure from it. She loved Lottie, and I rather suspected she thought the dog might be her mum. Did Lottie think of herself as Lulu's mother? No.

17

The White Cat

Apart from foxes, there was one animal Lottie had a particular animus for. The white cat. We never found out for sure where this beast lived, and I say beast advisedly because it terrorised Lulu, and I say for sure because we had a good idea but the owner would never admit it, for reasons I shall explain.

There was nothing about this animal's appearance that would tell you it had a nasty streak. It was actually quite attractive, sort of white with sort of a beige stripe down its spine. Actually, it was more attractive than I have perhaps been able to describe. However, they do say appearances can be deceptive, and in this case they are right, because this was one mean cat. Cats are pretty territorial, and Lulu is no exception. The white cat was also no exception, the difference being that it clearly considered everyone's garden to come within its own territory.

So Lulu would go out, the white cat would spot her and chase her back in. It drew the line at coming through the cat flap, whether because it had more sense or it was satisfied it had seen Lulu off I couldn't say. Of course what with Lulu throwing herself through the flap at a rate of knots and making a lot of noise while she was at it, that set Lottie off. She didn't know what she was barking at but she knew there was something wrong and she wanted to add her voice to the confusion.

Well, she quickly learned what was going on, because we taught her. If we saw the cat sunning itself on Liz's compost bin, or on the roof of the shed, all we had to do was call 'white cat' and Lottie tore from wherever she was, probably asleep, through the kitchen and down the garden ready to kill it. We soon learned that what with her being in a hurry to get out of the door we needed to be ready to open it so she wasn't held up.

This was quite a good game, and it gave Lottie exercise and kept her amused, so we didn't mind the white cat too much. Until, that was, the day Lulu came limping into the house with a gash in her side. Well, of course we couldn't be sure, but there was no doubt in our minds who the culprit was. I carried her gently out to the car and rushed to the vet, and one minor operation and £150 later she was on the mend.

This was too much though, so that evening I knocked on the door of the suspect's suspect house, just a few doors down the road. Oh no, they said, we don't have a white cat. Apparently un-neutered males can be aggressive, so I asked if any of their four cats was such and they said oh no, they had all been done. Well, I smelled a rat but what could I say?

Lottie never caught the cat, and for a long time the thing just kept coming back, so I think it learned that she couldn't, but on the other hand we did notice it had stopped coming into the garden after a while so maybe it had finally learned a lesson. Either that or it was indeed an un-neutered male and as a result of my call they had had him done. Or it had got run over in the road. We could only hope so. I mean the getting done thing, not the getting run over thing. You knew that.

18

Love Grows

Looking back on how our love grew for Lottie, a question arises. In fact it arose at the time but Liz and I viewed it differently. Well, that wasn't surprising. We viewed most things differently. The question was: did Lottie love us?

And this, I thought, came down to the different ways we looked at her. Liz anthropomorphised. I think, and I stress I don't know because what do I know, it came down to our different understanding not of dogs but of people. I don't profess to understand people, Liz does. I know I am a bad judge of character, she claims to be an excellent judge of character. Well, excuse me but if she was so good at it how come she made the mistake of marrying me? Anyway, I digress.

This is not a book about people, and yet understanding this dog of ours was of course a function not of her but of how the human brain works. I suppose a pointer here is the number of people, sadly, who buy a dog, perhaps because it's in fashion or perhaps because they think it will be good for the children, with no understanding that dogs are not small humans. They don't think like us and it is a horrible mistake to believe they do, that they should know what we want from them, that they will, for example, have some understanding of what we want from them. People, almost without exception, have some level of morality. No other animal does, and I'm no expert but I venture to suggest that apart from any physical characteristics this is the big thing that differentiates us from all the other animals. Of course other animals don't need morality, as far as I can see, what with it being an entirely human construct, but that is a much bigger subject and way, way outwith the purpose of this book.

Which brings to mind another issue, which I shall mention before I forget it. Liz is a practising Christian. I am a non-practising Jew. Now I can tell you that caused a number of problems, but the one I'm thinking of particularly is the Judeo-Christian view of animals. My understanding, which may well be faulty but bear with me, is that theists believe animals are subservient to us, that they are here to serve us. This, they believe, gives us the right to use them according to our own needs, not theirs, but that is straying beyond my topic as well, not to mention my competence.

A dog doesn't know what we want of it because it can't, and in that sense perhaps it is unfair of us even to keep dogs, and yet we started doing it, many thousands of years ago, because it was a symbiotic relationship that seemed to work. We got something from them and they got something from us. Fast forward to the twenty-first century and we get something from them but very often they have no idea what they are now supposed to do for us. They don't and can't think like us so that question doesn't even arise in their brains. Until we show a dog what we want it to do it cannot possibly know, and that makes it our responsibility, if they are going to be happy, to do that. And yes, owning a dog is a responsibility, not just to feed it well and care for its physical needs, but to understand it, or at least to try to understand it. And yes, to make it happy. I can see absolutely no reason to have a dog if we don't want to do that.

Look, there are shelfloads of books by people who know what they are talking about (as opposed to me) on dog psychology, so should I even be telling you this stuff? Well, it's my book and you are reading it so let's go with yes.

Liz complained frequently that Lottie loved me more than her, and that was almost certainly true. Liz walked her more than I did, but I played with her. Lottie didn't walk with us, so much as somewhere in the same vicinity. She is a loner, and walking her is not especially companionable. Playing with her, on the other hand, brought me into close contact with her and we connected, more as dogs than dog and human.

Liz, I suspected, could not get beyond the belief that Lottie should think like her. Look, I'm a human and I never understood her thought processes, so how could Lottie? Anyway, my point is that because Lottie couldn't think the way Liz wanted or expected her to, there was a breakdown in their relationship. Lottie probably loved her, but in her own way, not in a human way, and that wasn't enough for Liz. She loved Lottie, but in the same way she loved me. As long as Lottie and I met her expectations that was fine, but more often than not we didn't or couldn't, perhaps because we didn't know what they were. Love is unconditional, because if it's not then it's not actually love. Liz loved Lottie with certain conditions, and those conditions were never completely met. That wasn't Lottie's fault.

Liz and Lottie rubbed along well enough, and I will readily assert that Liz took care of the dog's physical needs in exemplary fashion, but still there was something missing, which was sad. It was especially sad when she said to me that despite everything she did for her Lottie didn't love her. Now if that is not anthropomorphising what is? What Liz meant was that Lottie didn't love her the way she wanted her to love her. Actually I think Lottie did love her in her own simple canine way. OK, she loved me too, and I suspect that was a different kind of love, perhaps because I'm a man and Lottie prefers men, perhaps for no other reason than that she is a woman, I mean a bitch.

While she was still young I had regularly got down on the floor for rough games with her (Lottie, not Liz), so it is possible that she saw me to some extent as another dog. Liz didn't do that. In fairness, rough games with Lottie were hard work and she wasn't really capable of that. Nonetheless, I rather think that unless and until you interact with a dog on their physical level, by which I mean heightwise but also doing the things they would do with their siblings growing up, a dog is not going to understand you as a dog and there is therefore going to be something missing in the relationship.

I daresay a dog trainer would argue with me here. They would say we are not dogs and dogs need to understand that, that we are the master in the relationship. Well they may be right, but on the other hand they might not be right. A dog expects the leader of the pack to be another dog. We expect it to make us humans the leader of the pack, but how reasonable is that? Yes, I might be wrong, but if I ever have another dog I shall, I'm afraid, be its father and its friend, not its owner.

19

Lonesome Dog

Most dogs like human company. All those thousands of years ago, when they adopted us as their companions, they self-developed for that trait. Working dogs, however, are first and foremost what we have bred them for, which is working, not being house pets. Shepherd dogs are definitely working dogs, and Carpathian Shepherds have been bred for sitting on a cold mountain all night guarding against wolves. That breeding doesn't make them ideal pets, and I have to say Lottie is not an ideal pet, if by ideal you mean sweet and cuddly and in your face.

Actually, she is very sweet and cuddly, when she wants to be; it's just that that isn't often, and in any case for her it's a learned characteristic. Stretched out on my sofa she was irresistible, and I did what any big softie would do, I cuddled her, and if she was in the mood she let me because something in her brain said that was good.

What she would not do is initiate contact. A bit like some women I have known. I don't think I have ever known her to come and ask for human company. Was that in her genes, or was it part of her psychological damage? I think perhaps a bit of both, but actually more the former. We had to accept that Lottie is a working dog who spends most of her time sleeping on one of our sofas. Actually, that's not as contradictory as it sounds, because any dog that is going to spend nights out on a cold mountain, listening and watching, ready to attack at short notice, is going to know to conserve its energy. Lottie is very good at conserving her energy. At any given time in the day, unless she is being fed or walked, she is asleep.

I think where Liz went wrong was believing that all this made Lottie stand-offish, and again that was probably her trying to apply human judgments to an animal that could not behave like a human. Lottie is what she is, and a happy relationship with her depends on understanding that, not constantly wishing she wasn't. In my long experience, people also are what they are, and expecting them to be otherwise tends to lead to disappointment.

And here I am going to digress and tell you something about Lottie, what with her being bred for nights on a Romanian mountain, you would not expect. It's that hating water thing I mentioned earlier. Once we got her used to going for walks she was always up for it, and like any normal dog she sat by the front door waiting to be let out. Unless it was raining. Lottie is a willful dog, and with her no means no. Could that be a fear of water? I really don't know. What is even stranger is that she would refuse to go out if it was raining but if she was already out and it started raining she didn't mind. It just didn't bother her. Now that I have never figured out. Trying to understand humans is hard, trying to understand dogs is harder, and trying to understand a rescued Carpathian Shepherd is more often than not a waste of time and effort.

And strangely she has one characteristic that is weirdly human. Well, by human I mean human and female. If I approached her, lying on her side on a sofa, and she didn't want my attention, she would roll over and show me her back, which left me in no doubt whatever that she didn't want to connect. Actually, I think that's pretty clever. I mean most dogs, as far as I know, will let you do almost anything and put up with it because, well, they are a dog and you are human. Not Lottie though. She knows how to say no and she isn't afraid to say it. If you don't like it, well, that's your problem. As I've said, Liz called that standoffishness, but that surely is a word for humans. Can it really be applied to a dog? Cats, definitely. Yes, cats are certainly standoffish. They are takers. They take and you give, and you keep giving, on demand, whether it's food or attention, and when they have had enough they simply walk away.

So perversely, we had a cat who thought she was a dog, and a dog who thought she was a cat. Can you blame me for being confused?

20

A Diagnosis

When we're sick, we like to have a diagnosis. It's reassuring to know that the doctor knows what's wrong with us and that our ailment has a name. Mind you, all too often that's as far as medicine goes but still, that's not the subject of this book.

So it was interesting, if not especially helpful, when the vet came up with a name for what troubled Lottie. Well, perhaps troubled is too strong a word. Once she settled on a routine it was nigh on impossible to break her of the habit. For example, we got into the habit of taking her into the recreation ground via the nearest gate, walking her right through and out of the farthest gate and then back home along the road. Walking on the pavement was something we particularly wanted to get her used to.

What we hadn't realised, though, by getting her used to this routine, was that it was the only routine she was going to be able to cope with. We tried to do the walk in reverse, go up to the far gate to walk back through the rec, but no, that was not what Lottie understood. In one gate and out of the other was what she understood. Fair enough, we were supposed to be in charge, and yes, we did make her understand that we made the rules, but those rules did not include putting her under unnecessary stress. So walks in the rec followed the same route every time.

The same issue applied when instead of turning out of the garden path onto the pavement for the rec we tried to turn left. A few hundred metres the other way was a pet shop. There was a distinct benefit to going that way, because it would get her used to going on the pavement and it would also get her used to going where we said we were going. And at the end of that trip was a pet shop where they had dog treats. Well, when a dog is as stressed as Lottie was by the time we finally got her there dog treats were an irrelevance.

We persisted with that one though, and after a few months she let us take her there, albeit reluctantly, and then the final breakthrough came when she took a treat from the pet shop owner. She was always, though, glad when we headed for home.

Anyway, I was going to tell you about the vet's diagnosis. Another clue is a very odd trait she had whenever we walked across a football or rugby pitch. She would walk along the white lines. And there you have it. Lottie, according to the vet, is autistic! Now I had never known that autism is a thing with dogs, and you probably didn't know it either, and for all I know this was a wild guess on the vet's part, except that the more we thought about it the more we came to see it. Was this anthropomorphising? Can a dog be autistic? Well, looking online there are certainly lots of articles that say this is a real diagnosis, although whether the diagnosis is actually helpful is a moot point. Mind you, I've already said that just giving a problem a name can be helpful, and giving Lottie's problem a name was in some way we didn't understand helpful. It was just that oh yes, now I understand moment. Plus of course the fact that if your problem has a name it means it's real. Well, it didn't matter of course whether anyone thought Lottie's problems were real. We knew they were. She didn't of course. Well, I say that, but how do we know what a dog is thinking? I'm not suggesting Lottie understood that she might be autistic, and anyway she's Romanian and I don't know what the Romanian for autism is.

Now, we were no longer tempted to say she was being awkward or willful. Well, I say we, but really I mean I. I may have mentioned this but Liz does tend to anthropomorphise, and she never quite accepted that Lottie had an excuse for her behaviour. Lottie didn't behave the way Liz wanted, or expected, because, well, partly because she is autistic (Lottie, not Liz) but also to be honest because she is a dog. Now I'm going to delve into an area of behaviour I have no qualifications for doing, partly because I am not a psychologist but also because what people think is pretty well a mystery to me. Men don't understand why women don't think like them, and women don't understand why men don't think like them. The problem, as I see it, is that these are unrealistic expectations.

It would be interesting to know whether dogs wonder why we humans don't think like them, but on reflection it's probably pointless wondering about that. As far as I know we know next to nothing about what dogs or any other animals think. We can observe their behaviour, in particular their reaction to our behaviour, and we can draw conclusions from those reactions, but those would be human conclusions, drawn from a human perspective. I don't think we can even begin to think like any animal other than ourselves. Look, if I as a man can't understand what women want, as they say, and women can't understand why I can't understand that, when let's face it we have the faculty of speech and we can tell each other stuff, what chance is there of dogs, or cats come to that, communicating their thoughts to humans and vice versa?

I'm an author, so for me language is important. My understanding, entirely from observation of myself, is that humans think in words. Whether we do that because we have developed language I have no idea. I expect someone does, but I don't. I am not an ologist of any kind. It just seems completely logical to me.

Now all animals can talk to other animals, of their own species, but can they talk to themselves, or would they need words to do that, because words describe things? I once watched a robin and a blackbird sitting in the same bush talking to each other, which was pretty amazing, and of course dogs talk to other dogs, but they don't talk to cats. And dogs (and all animals) communicate in ways that are not verbal at all, with behaviour and even smell. Yes, we also give off smells that some ancient part of our brain interprets, but we don't know we're doing it because we have lost the ability to understand those signals, perhaps because we have become so dependent on language.

All of which brings me back, thank goodness you say, to Lottie. The only way to understand what she was thinking was from the way she behaved, and by the same token the only way she could know what we were thinking (assuming, of course, she was interested to know), was from the way we behaved. We spoke to her, but as far as I understand it dogs don't have any idea what we're saying to them, they just pick up some notion from our tone of voice. So Lottie couldn't tell the difference between good girl and bad girl other than from the way we said it, which inevitably we did in a way that expressed what we were feeling. Had we said bad girl with a rising inflection, in a happy way, she would have taken that as approval.

We lie to each other, a lot in my experience and probably yours too, but we can't lie to a dog, because we can't hide what we're thinking when we speak to animals, and why would we? But can dogs lie to us? Could Lottie? It seems improbable, because as far as we know humans are the only animals that can think of the consequences of what they say. When a dog barks at another dog it means exactly what it's saying. All of which makes me wonder how we humans got ourselves into this muddle, how life became so complicated, but you will be pleased to know I am going to leave that train of thought there.

21

It's a Dog's Life

Why do we say it's a dog's life to mean it's a bad life? Good grief, what would I give to be fed regularly, taken for walks and have my every need attended to? Not to mention loved. But more than any of that would be the relief to get off the treadmill of the ridiculous lives we create for ourselves.

Both Lottie and Lulu have pretty cushy lives. They get all of the above but, as I say, they don't have to think about anything or worry about anything. They don't have to make plans and arrangements. They don't actually have to do anything. Lulu especially has it easy. Lottie, after all, might not want to go for a walk when Liz says let's go. Yes, I know that would be abnormal for a dog, but I think you understand by now that Lottie is abnormal. Sometimes she doesn't want to go for a walk. Like, for example, if it's raining. Or if ... well, she just doesn't. That's a strange one by dog standards, but sometimes she just doesn't want to go, for no apparent reason. And sometimes she doesn't want to eat. Most dogs are pretty keen on food but Lottie is not only a picky eater but she's also a moody eater. The feeling just has to be right. She can even do that cat thing.

You know, sniff at the food and walk away, as if to say come on people, this isn't what I was expecting. You would think a dog found fending for itself on the mean streets of Targoviste, then dumped in a massive kennel where she had to compete at feeding time, would eat anything it was given, whenever it was available, but not our Lottie.

Liz said this is ridiculous, all the dog behaviourists say offer them the food and if they don't eat it pick it up and they can go hungry. They will, they say, soon learn not to turn their noses up. Well, those dog behaviourists are surely right, except for one thing. They haven't met Lottie.

So I did what I was told and picked her bowl up, and then when Lottie came into the kitchen later in the evening I surreptitiously put it back down. Was this allowing a dog to tell me what to do? Possibly, but here again I have to remind you of something I've said before. Lottie was from working stock. She was bred to be up and alert all night. She preferred to sleep out in the garden at night. Would it be all that surprising if she wanted to eat before going on shift? Was it actually fair for us to insist she follow our routine rather than obey her inbred instincts?

Which all raises a question about the millions of dogs out there, normal by Lottie's standards, who are having their lives circumscribed by their human owners, because that's what the books say, or it's convenient and it's only a dog, but come on, I make no claim to know what's in a dog's mind but I can do what I do all day in my day job, which is analyse a situation and find solutions. And my analysis of the lives most pet dogs lead is that they might look cushy but actually they are nigh on unnatural. OK, it's unnatural for any dog to live in a house with central heating and food laid on twice a day so it doesn't have to hunt, but ... well actually I don't have a but. It's just unnatural.

Was I overthinking Lottie? Well, I might as well tell you I overthink most things. It gets me into trouble, always has. But Lottie? No, I don't think so. I had brought her into my world (well, Liz had brought her into her world, but still) and that was not the end, it was the beginning. The beginning of learning from her, figuring her out, in part because of her psychological problems but also because she is a dog. I have had dogs before and did I agonise over them like I did with her? Actually, I don't remember, but I suspect not. That is probably in part just a function of getting older, or in my case old, but also because Lottie was the first dog I had ever been faced with who had the kind of problems that opened a window into the life of dogs. She was, in human terms, special needs. My daughter teaches special needs children, something I could not do, but what I was doing with Lottie was much the same. My daughter thinks I'm a bit odd for writing a book about a dog, but then she thinks I'm odd anyway.

Could I help other troubled dogs? Probably not because after all I am not a specialist in this field. My relationship with Lottie grew out of her needs which coincided with mine, her need to be loved and my need to love. It was serendipitous, I suppose.

Which made it all the more gut-wrenching to have to say goodbye to her.

22

Barking Mad

All dogs bark when someone comes into their home. It's completely normal. But is it what we think it is? I had always accepted it as protecting their territory, as probably does everyone, but there was something about Lottie's behaviour in this regard that cast some doubt on that assumption.

Lottie was a fearful dog. She is less fearful now, but it will never go away completely. A knock at the door makes her bark frantically, as you would expect, but there is something in her demeanour as she barks that suggests something other than pure territoriality is going on. There is also fear. We have always seen it in her.

This was demonstrated especially when we let the visitor in. If Lottie was upstairs, which she more often than not was, she would come to the top of the stairs, creep down a little to get a good look at them, and bark frantically as they came into the entrance hall, again not surprisingly, but what we could see in her was that she was afraid of the visitor. But was she afraid in the sense that she was concerned that a stranger was coming into her space, or was she simply afraid, not for the house, not for the property of her owners, but for herself? It did look like she wasn't protecting the house, she was protecting herself.

Now not being an expert I cannot say whether this was peculiar to Lottie or in fact it's what is going on in the minds of all dogs when they bark at visitors. Having said that, a lot of dogs bark but they wag their tails while they are barking, which suggests they are happy to see the visitor and barking is just another way of showing their excitement. Lottie didn't wag her tail, she tucked it down under her bottom. This was fear, and it was almost certainly fear for herself.

If we let the visitor in and, say, took them through to the living room or the kitchen, Lottie would do two things. First she would go and curl up on the sofa in my office upstairs. What was she thinking? We couldn't know that, but Lottie is a deep thinker and she was probably doing that, trying to process information, assess risk, come to terms with the situation.

Because very often what she would then do, after a while, was go downstairs to inspect the visitor. She did this silently, sometimes without us even noticing. She would sit down in front of them, just looking, which most people found pretty unnerving. She sat silently and didn't bark unless they moved, or they went to stand up from their seat, so most people decided not to do either of those things until we removed Lottie. She never went for anyone of course. This was psychological warfare, and it usually resulted in a win for the dog.

When a dog attacks it is out of fear, attack being the

best defence. The difference with Lottie was the curling up on the sofa thing first. Was she plotting her next move, or was she just gathering her courage?

Once she started taking treats, we tried a new idea, which worked pretty well. The visitor was given a treat to give her in the hallway, and this way we did have some success showing her that strangers in the house could be a good thing. Providing, of course, the visitor had the courage to do it, which not everyone did.

After a while she developed a new tactic. If we had friends to dinner, she would wait until we were all seated and she would come and lie down at the feet of one of our visitors. We had a couple we regularly invited and the wife was somewhat nervous of Lottie. Whether she was nervous so Lottie knew to intimidate her or the intimidation made her nervous I don't know, but this couldn't go on, so we removed Lottie upstairs when she did this. But we never thought to shut her away, so before long she crept down and did it again. I don't know about the dogs of war but Lottie is the dog of psychological warfare.

I have never been afraid of her, but on the other hand I never took her for granted. A domesticated wild animal, remember. If she did get a bit carried away I would always make it very clear she had crossed a line. I don't remember ever smacking her, partly because I'm not keen on that as a way of training dogs and partly because the last thing a fearful dog needs is physical violence. Smacking her would have been a betrayal of trust. And in any case, why would you hurt the one you love?

23

Touching

Humans have a need to touch, and dogs and cats, I think, are incredibly important in that they give us a reason to do that without having to make excuses.

I'm a tactile person. I hug my grown up sons when I see them, which in fairness is only about once a year what with them living abroad, and they are completely happy with that (the hugging thing, not the once a year thing). I grew up in a family where no-one ever touched anyone else (yes, strange, I know) but I soon learned how it's done. Touching your children, your lover, kissing a friend on the cheek, shaking hands, just putting a hand on someone's arm when you talk to them, these are all important ways we connect with others. Is it therefore surprising if one of the reasons we have a dog or a cat is to have something to satisfy the need for physical contact?

And dogs like to be touched. They are happy to be stroked. Well, when I say dogs I'm excluding Lottie, because she is not tactile. When she turns her back on you it's tempting to ask if it's something you said, but of course that would be ridiculous. In case I haven't mentioned it, Lottie is very beautiful. She has a long shaggy coat, and the urge to stroke her is often overwhelming. Well, overwhelming might be a little strong but you know what I mean. I don't know if the same applies with short-haired dogs, but it's just instinctive to stroke her, and why would anyone not follow an instinct like that?

Actually, if you are a cat lover you will know that they too love to be stroked, and I don't know if Lottie had spoken to Lulu about this but Lulu also doesn't always want to be stroked, or picked up, or cuddled. What's wrong with these animals? That just left Liz, and she too didn't much go in for that sort of thing, so I know what you're thinking, the three women in my life weren't tactile, and guess who they weren't tactile with. Uhuh, maybe it wasn't them, maybe it was me.

Or maybe not. Apart from Liz, the other two were strays. Maybe they had learned to be independent of humans too much to need them now. Yes, I expect it was nothing more than that.

When you think about it, a dog has only two ways to touch. It can lick you and it can bite you. Look, I know you are probably starting to wonder what I saw in Lottie, what with her not doing all the things normal dogs do, but bear with me. Maybe by the time we get to the end of this book you will understand. I can't recall her ever licking me, now I think back on the three years I spent with her. And the only way she ever used her bite was if I was brushing her coat. If I caught a snag in her hair, or if she had just had enough of it, on account of her having a low boredom threshold, she would take my hand in her mouth, gently, to say enough. I always respected that, partly on account of respecting Lottie but also because when a dog with big teeth puts them round your hand you ignore what it is saying at your peril.

At the risk of convincing you this dog really was not normal at all, I might as well tell you at this point that another thing Lottie didn't do was wag her tail. She just is not a tail wagger. She's only got half a tail anyway, but I really don't see how that would make any difference. The instinct just isn't there. Does that mean she isn't ever happy? No, absolutely not. What it means, I suggest, is that she experiences happiness in a way that most dogs don't. Happiness for Lottie is more a kind of contentment than a kind of joy. OK, maybe I have just contradicted myself. Maybe it's true that she doesn't feel joy. Most dogs are simple. If they like something it makes them happy, and they respond by wagging their tail. It's how we know they are happy. We know people are happy because they smile. A person who claims to be happy but never smiles would probably be unconvincing. So you might think we couldn't know that Lottie was happy, but we really could.

Before she became what I now think of as normal, which means normal for her, not normal normal, we always knew when she was unhappy. Her tail would go down, right down, and it would stay there. As she developed with us the one thing we always commented on was her tail. What angle it was at was a sure way for us to know what she was feeling. Right down meant unhappy and probably frightened (I shall come back in due course to what made Lottie frightened), right up meant relaxed, and horizontal meant she was thinking about it.

On a walk, if her tail was straight up or even somewhere between there and horizontal, we knew she was relaxed. And relaxed was a very big issue. Relaxed was good enough. In fact it was what we aimed for with her. She came to us terribly stressed, so relaxed was more than good enough. In fact, it would not be going too far to say that for Lottie relaxed was happiness. Yes, it didn't happen a lot but it did happen more and more, that she was relaxed, and then we knew we had rescued her. Well, you might think bringing her from the mean streets of Romania to a cushy life in England was rescuing her but she was not truly rescued until she was happy.

And the more time she spent with her tail up rather than down, the more rescued she was.

24

Coming home

Some dogs, I am led to believe, suffer from separation anxiety. They can't cope with being left alone in the house for long periods. They become stressed and can display that stress in destructive behaviour. I've never had a dog like that, or perhaps I've never left a dog for long periods. Not sure about that one.

And Lottie certainly benefited from us, or one of us at least, being in the house most of the time. There were short periods when we left her, for example the highlight of our week, coffee at Waitrose followed by the weekly shopping. I know, it's a bit sad, but hey, we were pensioners, what do you expect? So did being left alone bother her? No, it did not. How do we know that? Because when we went out she was probably sleeping on one of the sofas, and when we got back it was quite obvious she hadn't moved.

That was the good side of that bit of her personality, but there was a bad side as well. Actually, I didn't think it was a bad thing but Liz did. All dogs, whether they suffer from separation anxiety or not, are pleased to see their family come home. They run up and wag their tail and make a fuss of them. Did Lottie do any of those things? Well, no. She might have raised an eyebrow when she heard the key in the lock but we wouldn't know that.

Liz found this very unsatisfactory, on account of it's not what dogs are supposed to do. I can't say it bothered me. I never found it hard to accept any of Lottie's foibles. She is what she is. Wishing she would be something else, say like normal dogs, would be pointless. (In a long and sorry life I have found pretty well consistently that just wishing for things to happen tends to lead to disappointment.) It wouldn't change her, and greeting us when we got home wasn't something we could teach her. I do think that in her own quiet way she was pleased when we came back. She just didn't show her feelings. Liz wanted her, very much, to show her feelings, so on second thoughts perhaps Lottie didn't really have feelings.

Actually, I think that is true. Lottie has always been a solitary dog. That's not just because of her problems, or even perhaps connected with them. I have always thought it's part of her genetic inheritance. Dogs that are bred for spending solitary nights on cold mountains are not going to be happy waggy pets.

Anyway, I was instructed not to go up to say hello to Lottie when we came in. If she couldn't be bothered to come down we were not going to go to her. That was the theory, based on what all dogs should be like. Well, if I had to go upstairs, say to take my shoes off, who was to know if I said hello to her? And the funny thing was she always let me know she was pleased to see me. Not happy waggy pleased, just happy in her own Carpathian way. It didn't bother me in the slightest that I had to go to her instead of her coming to me. I didn't need her to be like other dogs. Of course it is possible, no probable, that I needed to see her more than she needed to see me, but so what? If I had obeyed the instruction not to say hello to her, who was going to be the loser? Not Lottie.

Even now, two years since I left, Liz still wants Lottie to greet her when she comes home, and very occasionally I get a report that she has done just that. I'm pleased, for Liz, but also for Lottie. I can't be with her, and I shall never see her again, and part of me wishes I didn't get reports about her, but for now I do, and I am filled with love for her and if she is happy then I am happy. Well, not happy for me but happy for her.

25

Bath Time

I think two things are axiomatic. The first is that dogs get dirty, and the second is that they are perfectly happy to remain dirty and will resist all attempts to wash them. Of course it could be the other way round, that they don't like being washed and so are happy to stay dirty, like little boys. Whether I was one of those little boys I don't remember, but if I was something changed because Liz regularly complained about the amount of time I spent in the shower.

Anyway, I was going to tell you about Lottie, not me. We didn't wash her very regularly, partly because she really really did not like the shower (there are two showers but no bath in the house) but also because it entailed a massive amount of effort on our part. Sometimes, though, a dog's got to do what a dog's got to do.

The first effort was me carrying her up two flights of stairs. I don't know why two, because there is a shower on the first floor, but that wasn't for me to question. And I can tell you carrying a twenty-three kilo Carpathian Shepherd who knows exactly what you're up to, and really does not concur, up two flights of stairs is not at all easy.

Then it was my job to push her into the shower, where Liz was waiting stripped to her underwear, and dog and woman fought it out. All I had to do was watch the entertainment from outside, towel in hand (for Lottie not Liz; she could sort herself out). And of course, as every dog owner knows they don't run outside into the garden to shake themselves off, they do it the instant you release them, in this case in our bedroom. She did look sweet, though, when she came out of the shower (Lottie, not Liz), and even though she always knew what was coming and always fought it, she never held a grudge for having been put through the ordeal. That, I imagine, is a dog thing, not holding a grudge. I'd like to say it's only humans, but in my experience it might also be cats. Yes, with cats it is always a psychological contest, but dogs, bless them, are simpler creatures. Some people (and cats) put that down to them being a bit unintelligent, but is there actually any evolutionary advantage to resentment? Could we not learn a thing or two from dogs? I speak in general terms, what with me being the kind of bloke who definitely holds a grudge, but that doesn't concern you.

So there was Lottie, clattering down two flights of stairs having had a good shake in the bedroom first, and straight out into the garden to roll in the earth and get rid of the smell of dog shampoo. There probably was a reason for washing her, but what was it? Still, it's the principle of the thing and, as mothers of little boys might say, perhaps fresh dirt is better than old dirt.

And here is something I have often wondered, what with having a dog and a cat. Cats spend a lot of time washing themselves but dogs don't do it at all. Why is that? Of course, dogs and cats are associated with each other in our minds because they are both domestic pets, but there is absolutely no reason why they should resemble each other in that or any other respect. Actually, thinking about this, a better question might be, given that dogs don't feel the need to wash themselves (and why would they?) why do cats? Why, for cats, is it an imperative? There is no part of itself a cat cannot wash, including its face and the back of its neck. Cats are fussy, or so it seems to us. Dogs are wonderfully unfussy. Mud on a dog's coat is simply not an issue, whereas a cat can be seen washing parts of itself that are not dirty - to the human eye. And that's another thing. Given that cats can't see the dirt, how do they know it's there? How does a cat feel dirty? Questions, questions, all of which are sure to have answers if you know about these things, which obviously I don't.

Coming back to Lottie, we were conscious that a dog has natural oils on its coat that one really shouldn't wash off, which is a good reason for showering infrequently but not a reason for not showering at all. If a dog is going to live in our home, it does have to behave just a little like a human. In Lottie's case with her spending so much time outdoors in all weathers, her natural oils naturally serve an important function.

And by all weathers I do not mean rain, as already mentioned, I mean cold and wind and even snow.

The first winter we had her it snowed a little. It only ever snows a little nowadays, what with the climate changing which I won't go into, but the first time she went out in the stuff she was overcome with delight. Here at last was something resembling the Carpathian Mountains. Lottie has never worn one of those dog coats that small dogs, and even some big dogs, seem to find necessary, because she has a wonderful coat of her own, the gift of her genetic inheritance.

She also tended to eat more in the winter and therefore put on a little weight, which Liz worried about but I reasoned was quite normal for a working dog. Her coat is good protection, but she also needs a layer of fat to fend off the cold. She always loses it in the spring, which surely means I am right about that.

So, Lottie and snow. It will remain one of my fondest memories of her, watching her childlike pleasure in rolling in it and running along digging it up with her snout. And here's another thought, if you can bear another one. We know what snow is and where it comes from, but for a dog, well, it gets up in the morning, goes out into the garden and what was green yesterday is now white. Don't they wonder why? No, I suppose not. Wondering why is, I suppose, one of the many things that makes us human and led us to develop way beyond all the other animals, until we started not just to wonder why but why not, and that turned out to be dangerous, but I'll leave that there before I go off completely at a tangent.

Lulu, however, did not like snow, so perhaps cats do wonder why. Why was it grass yesterday but today it's cold and wet and nasty and necessitates you picking your way carefully through it to find somewhere to go to the toilet? This does make it seem like, yes, cats are more thoughtful, even more intelligent, than dogs, but perhaps that is anthropomorphising. Perhaps there is actually nothing particularly clever about not liking snow, and even wondering what it's doing there. Perhaps, and here I accept I am going out on a limb, it is more intelligent just to enjoy it. Perhaps dogs have an evolutionary advantage over us, one we like to denigrate because we think we rule the planet. Perhaps not asking too many questions is part of the reason for the success of dogs. Actually, I did say I would leave the question alone, so apologies.

To say that Lottie was not thoughtful would be quite wrong, and of course the same would apply to every other dog. Having said that, when I watch a spaniel chasing inanely after the same ball time after time, I do wonder about dog intelligence, but on the other hand a spaniel is a working dog and if the only work its owner can give it to do is running after a ball and bringing it back for hours on end, well, that probably says more about the intelligence of people than their dogs.

Oh, and one more thing about snow while I'm thinking about it. The first time we took Lottie out in it, after a while she started limping. Naturally, we inspected her paws to see if she had trodden on something sharp and cut herself, which she had done before, but that wasn't it. It was the snow. As she walked, the snow under her feet melted a little and compacted in a hard ball. This was so hard it hurt her to walk, indeed it was so hard we couldn't remove it without cutting away the fur under her paws, between her pads. The snow had combined with the fur, so there was no other choice. It brought immediate relief, but it posed a question we couldn't answer. How can a dog that is bred for working in snow have fur under its paws that quickly makes it impossible to walk? It was a riddle that just didn't make sense. It still doesn't, and Lottie has to have a haircut under her paws when it snows. Strange, very strange.

26

Here be Snakes

Having a dog is similar to having children, in that you never stop worrying. There always seems to be something to angst about, sometimes serious and sometimes not so serious but you worry anyway. There is of course, the main worry, which is their health, and Lottie was seriously damaged when she came to us so for the first year there was lots to deal with, but even after that, although she was a strong dog, we remained anxious about her physical wellbeing. And then of course there was her mental health. Sometimes we just thought her funny and quirky and we didn't angst unnecessarily about her strange ways, and sometimes there were more serious issues that we couldn't laugh off.

But perhaps the most serious worry was adders. An adder can kill a human, so it can certainly kill a dog, and where we walked Lottie on the Downs there were a lot of them. I have only once seen one, and I don't mind admitting I don't like snakes. Who does? We live in a country where most people never see a snake in their whole life, and it's this lack of familiarity that increases our fear of them. Liz grew up in east Africa, so she at least had a little experience of them.

The Downs are ideal adder country, and there were signs put up by the council warning walkers to be wary of them, which tells you how serious the problem was. Talking to other dog walkers, there were always stories of a dog that had been bitten. The advice, if your dog is bitten, is to immobilise it to reduce the spread of the poison, and get it to a vet as quickly as possible. Well, if you are three miles from where you parked, and your twenty-three kilo dog does get bitten, how are you going to carry it to your car? It would have been hard enough for me, but if Liz was walking Lottie on her own it would have been impossible.

Dogs naturally sniff around in long grass, and that is exactly where an adder is likely to be sunning itself, and the first thing it is going to do when it's disturbed by a curious dog is to attack. (Adders, by the way, are a protected species, so if one does attack your dog you are not allowed to kill it. I can tell you, though, that if one had ever threatened my dog I would have shot first and asked questions later. No, I don't carry a shotgun on dog walks. It's just an expression.)

We couldn't stop Lottie exploring, and neither would we have wanted to, so all that left was to have a plan of action prepared in case it happened. Luckily, she is a wary dog, so unless she came across a snake unexpectedly we did at least have the comfort of believing she would not have pestered one if she found it. Unlike, say, a spaniel of my acquaintance, which would not know the meaning of caution when faced with something it didn't recognise. Things you don't recognise, if you are that particular spaniel (and spaniels generally as far as I know), are a reason for sticking your nose in.

Our emergency protocol involved packing an old sheet in the capacious dog-walking bag Liz always carried, and an antidote to the poison, and some wishful thinking that in a moment of panic we would administer the antidote, get Lottie on the stretcher, and run like mad for the car. If it ever did happen, Liz would probably have been more cool-headed than me. The plan assumed the vet would have both the knowledge and the drugs to deal with such an emergency, but we reckoned that was likely. Well, we hoped so anyway. I would have driven there, because Liz's driving frightened me anyway, even when there was no dying dog on the back seat.

Luckily, the emergency never happened. After Liz and I split up, it worried me for a while that she would be walking on her own on the Downs, but eventually you understand there is nothing you can do and you put it out of your mind. It's like your children. When they grow up and leave home you can't imagine them coping with life without you, but they do and you let them get on with it. I worried when my younger son told me about snakes and scorpions on his army base, but he didn't seem scared so I tried not to be. I try not to think about Lottie, which is manifestly ridiculous because how else could I write about her? Well, the truth is I did try not to think about her, then when I found I couldn't do that I decided to write about her, and then I stopped doing this because it was hurting, and then I decided to tell the story, right through to the end, hoping, perhaps, that I could get her out of my mind.

I shall let you know, at the end of the book, if that was a success.

(By the way, the Council gave planning permission for a housing development on the edge of the Downs, where they become Brighton, and they collected up all the adders on the site and re-homed them in the very place where Lottie and lots of other dogs walk every day. Adders, it seems, have more rights than dogs.)

27

Lost and Found

One of the worst things that can happen to any dog lover, other, of course, than the object of their love dying, is the dog getting lost. Every time I see some notice about a lost dog I can imagine the anguish of its owners. That, though, cannot be as bad as the anguish a dog suffers when it is lost. We at least can do something – not only looking but asking other people to look. A lost dog, in my experience, panics and goes round in circles looking for its owners. It is perhaps impossible to imagine what goes through the dog's mind in that situation, but it is hardly difficult to imagine how dreadful it is. We are dependent on our dogs, but that is as nothing against the dependence they have on us. To be honest, I don't even want to think about it.

It happened more than once with Lottie, and unlike most dogs she was at a serious disadvantage, because she never barked to attract our attention. I have no idea why not, but she just didn't have that instinct. Lottie is not a communicator, as you will by now understand, and barking to make contact with us simply is not in her repertoire of canine behaviour. Perhaps that comes from being lost on the streets of Targoviste in Romania. Perhaps she lost her mother and barked for her but her mother never came and found her. That, too, does not bear thinking about, so I shan't.

Lottie got lost in various ways and in various circumstances. If she chased the white cat up the alley by the side of the house, she would disappear for a while but eventually she did come back, more often than not. The not part was when she wriggled through a gap in the hedge to get through to the recreation ground behind the house. I couldn't do that, so I had to run round to the entrance and hope she hadn't strayed too far. I can tell you, every time I had to do that I was filled with dread. Indeed, sometimes I didn't find her for quite a while, and every minute that passed was agony. You can't know, in that situation, if your dog really has run off, and you are never going to see her again.

That was particularly nasty one evening when I took her for her last walk of the day round the rec. At the far end, I was distracted by something and when I looked down she wasn't there. I shone the torch into the bushes, I called, I panicked, but not one of things helped in any way. I didn't want to leave the rec, obviously because she might appear at any moment and not find me, but I took a chance and ran home to enlist Liz and our neighbour to join the search. Well, she did eventually appear, from where none of us could see, and she had no idea what all the fuss was about. Did we scold her? No. What would have been the point? She didn't know the anguish she had caused, so telling her off would have achieved nothing.

As an aside, I do think that sometimes people chastise

their dog without considering that the dog doesn't actually know what they have done wrong (or indeed that crime and punishment are a thing they need to understand). People also do that with their children, but at least a child has some chance of understanding why it is being reprimanded. A dog rarely does. In any case, what we consider a crime is probably nothing of the kind to a dog. Lottie couldn't know the grief she had caused me, so nothing I could do was going to teach her not to do it again. Which she did, more than once.

After this episode, though, I had the bright idea of buying her one of those flashing collars, and I can tell you it was a tremendous relief that I could follow where she was going in the dark. You might, by the way, be thinking that the best way to stop her running off would have been to keep her on a lead, and I know many people do walk their dog on a lead, but to be honest I have never seen the point. Apart from in situations where it is a necessity, for example near a road, or where there are livestock, a dog on a lead is first of all not getting the exercise it needs and second of all it can't do the things it needs to do like sniffing and exploring. A dog on a lead is, to be honest, an extension of its owner and of its owner's needs, just like a dog that becomes obsessed with chasing and retrieving a ball is, fair enough, getting exercise, but it is man-made exercise. Wild dogs don't chase balls, and cave-dwellers' dogs didn't either. Come on people, think like a dog. When a dog is off lead it is doing what dogs do, using all its instincts and all its brain functions to do those things. A dog chasing a ball over and over is, well, a toy.

So I am rather happy that Lottie never did that, even though, in all honesty, we did, in our ignorance at the time, try to encourage her.

Anyway, back to the subject of her getting lost. The very first time was when we took her to the pony field, which is not so much a field as a fenced-off scrubby area where the council puts wild ponies. I expect there is a reason for that. Anyway, at first we kept her on the training lead, which is five metres long, so she could explore and sniff but she couldn't get away. Then, one day, with not a little trepidation, we took her off the lead. The field is securely enclosed (because of the ponies probably), so we knew she couldn't go too far, but still, it's about half a mile long, so there was plenty of hiding she could do if she was so minded. One side of the field is a very steep slope down, covered in trees and bushes, and naturally Lottie made a dash for it. So far not too bad, but when she didn't reappear after a few minutes the worry set in. In the end, I scrambled down the slope, (with some difficulty, but not with as much difficulty as scrambling up again) to look for her, only to find she had run up the slope further along and was quite uninterested in us.

Looking back on that episode, when time after time she went down to investigate and we didn't give it a thought, it was hard to remember just how worried we had been. Watching Lottie grow up was pretty much like watching a child grow up. There are heart-stopping moments, and there are times when you look back on those moments and smile to yourself for being so anxious.

I should say the worst episode we ever had was out on the South Downs. We were walking with some friends, not, perhaps, giving Lottie enough attention. We rounded a corner with her and she came face to face with a very large, very black dog. I say very black, because Lottie has never had an issue with large dogs (it's small ones she doesn't like) but she is weirdly sensitive to colours. She likes dogs with her own colouring (black and tan) but she has a particular dislike for black ones. Anyway, there was this big black dog and Lottie was gone. None of us saw which direction she ran off in and the terrain was such that spotting her more than fifty metres away was going to be very difficult. Well, we searched, we called, we scanned as far as we could with our bird-watching binoculars, but it looked hopeless. The minutes passed, and it seemed like an hour passed too but actually it didn't.

The wonderful thing about dog lovers is that if they know yours is lost they understand immediately the necessity and the urgency of helping you. They know you would do it for them. And that was how we retrieved her. Another dog walker found her, put her on their lead, and brought her back to us.

It was after this fiasco that I came up with the excellent idea of getting a satellite tracker for Lottie. Yes, there really are such things. Somewhere out in geostationary orbit a satellite would be able to find Lottie and show us on a cellphone within a few metres where she was. There was only one problem. I don't use a cellphone. Liz does, though, and for whatever reason she thought my brilliant idea was not brilliant at all, possibly because it was my idea, and so we never did it. Could I have got a cellphone just for that purpose? Yes, but as I knew I wasn't going to be with Lottie for much longer there seemed little point.

(You might or might not want to know why I don't have a cellphone. Am I a Luddite? No. I don't even know where Ludd is. People ask me how I manage without one, to which my answer is very simple. I have never found a use for one. And while I'm at it, why don't I, like everyone in the United Kingdom, call it a mobile? That's because a mobile is something you hang over a baby's cot, not a telephone. I have always thought the American word - cellphone but not 'cell', which is ridiculous - is a far better description of what the device is and how it works. Well, there you have it. Strange, perhaps, and I probably could not argue with you.)

Incidental to my story, I'll tell you something strange that happened one night while I was in the rec with Lottie. We had just arrived so she was still on the lead. I looked up from her and there was a fox, just sitting, seemingly doing nothing. That in itself was not surprising. The foxes tended to watch Lottie and only run away when she gave chase (she never caught one; she's not a fast runner, which always made me wonder if foxes like a game of chase). What was surprising was that just a few metres away from the fox was a cat, also seemingly just sitting there doing nothing. What they were in fact doing, the fox and the cat, was enjoying each other's company. How or why, don't ask me, but it was happening for sure, and it gave the lie to the claim that foxes are a threat to domestic cats. Anyway, Lottie soon broke up their little party.

Lottie may be a little short sighted, I suspect. She would chase cats in the rec, although never very seriously, but on more than one occasion she chased what she presumably thought was a cat but it was just a plastic carrier bag blowing in the wind. As soon as she realised her mistake, she would walk off casually, trying not to look foolish, hoping no-one had seen her. Perhaps it was not so much short-sightedness as poor night vision, although given her breeding that would be surprising. Mind you, she could always tell the difference, even in the dark, between Lulu and any other cat, because she never chased Lulu.

And it is just possible she is hard of hearing. Liz bought one of those special whistles that make a very high-pitched sound that dogs are supposed to respond to. All I can say is that either Lottie couldn't hear it or she could but she didn't know what it meant or she could hear it and she knew what it meant but she didn't care. I do wonder, if dogs can hear it, how they are supposed to know it means come here. I mean, why should they? In any case it was not of the slightest help. Actually, come to think of it, when we blew it none of the other dogs around responded either, so on reflection I think it's just another one of those things that are supposed to work but don't.

28

Upstairs Downstairs

One of Lottie's favourite places to sleep, during the day at least, is on the stairs from the ground floor to the first floor, where the staircase goes round a bend, which gives her a bigger space to lie on. I suspect this might be because from that vantage point she can watch the whole of the front hall and the front door, while keeping her distance in case she needs to escape. In fact, now I think about it, she would lie there, often not sleeping at all but just lying with her eyes open. Watching, presumably. Is that a Lottie thing or a guard dog thing?

It used to annoy Liz, whereas I, naturally, carefully stepped over her. Lulu, though, was another matter. Lottie would be facing down the stairs, so if the cat wanted to go up she couldn't. She wasn't so much afraid of Lottie as respectful, which was probably wise. If she was above Lottie, she could tell the dog couldn't see her and the idea of jumping clean over her was terribly tempting, and actually on one occasion she did just that. For a small cat with a limp, that was impressive. Lulu. I miss her too.

Upstairs was always Lottie's safe space. If she couldn't

take a bone or a treat out into the garden she always ran upstairs with it. Again, that might be her fearfulness manifesting itself, but perhaps not, perhaps all wild animals prefer to eat away from prying eyes, and a dog, as I have said before, is a domesticated wild animal. It's one reason why I was happy for her to eat in the garden, because that was very obviously what she wanted to do. I never forgot how we had to feed her when she first arrived, in the living room with the door closed. On reflection, it is possibly more a Lottie thing than just a dog thing. And Lottie is a slow eater, compared, at least, with a Labrador I know, although Labradors are notoriously fast eaters. If a piece of meat gets pushed out of the bowl, she will pick that up before carrying on, which I always found a little surprising. Slow and methodical, our Lottie.

As well as the first flight of stairs Lottie also liked sometimes to sleep at night at the top of the stairs up to our bedroom in the loft. Now that was something we had to watch out for, because falling over her and tumbling down the stairs was always something we had to be wary of. If she is lying where she wants to be, it's actually quite hard to persuade her to move, possession being nine tenths of the law as far as she is concerned. How she knows that I can't say. Perhaps it's what they say in Romania too.

To us humans the stairs were just the bit from one storey to another, but to Lottie they were part of her domain, a place in and of themselves. If anyone came to the front door, unlike most dogs she would bark not at the door but from the stairs. Protecting them or the first floor, or more likely protecting herself, watching from a good vantage point but with a well-understood escape route.

And given that her coat sheds, a lot, it made the stairs the hardest part of the house to clean. Actually, that's quite funny, because the dog Liz had decided we would get was going to be small, and it was not going to shed. What we got was Lottie, too big for her to pick up, and needing constant grooming.

Inevitably, it fell to me to do that. Did I mind? Brushing her coat was only ever a pleasure. Liz being Liz, we bought all sorts of combs and brushes that promised to be the ideal grooming tool, and surprise surprise most of them weren't, but in the moulting season she (Lottie, not Liz) had to be groomed more or less every day, if only to reduce the amount of hair she deposited everywhere. It was hard to say if she actually enjoyed it but she certainly tolerated it, until I snagged a tangled bit and then she let me know she wasn't happy. She has long hair growing on her hind legs and that did get pretty tangled, so I had to be careful there. Her way of letting me know she had had enough was to roll over onto her back to make it much harder to reach the bits I wanted to brush. I wonder if most dogs would simply run away when they had had enough, but I always groomed her on one of the sofas and she was never going to relinquish her place just like that.

You might think I indulged her too much, but actually I'm not quite as soft as I probably sound. Lottie, remember, came to us very damaged. Not just ordinarily damaged but with serious mental health problems. As she settled down and became more normal, what we called 'more dog', it would have been easy to forget where she had been and what she had come through to get this far. I am quite certain, if you are a dog trainer, that you will say my approach was wrong, that I fell in love with her and that blinded me to the correct way to teach a dog, but I am going to beg to differ, and on account of this being my book, and Lottie being my dog, I claim the right to do that. Her first professional trainer made the mistake of thinking he could ignore her problems and just do what he did with every other dog but he was proved wrong. I'm not saying Lottie is the only dog who had ever been mentally damaged by a rough start in life, but I am saying she is the only such dog who had the good or bad fortune (take your pick) to come into my life. Whilst I will readily admit to being pretty clueless when it comes to people, with Lottie there was a connection that is hard, if not impossible, to describe. I'm not saying a lot of dog owners don't also have that connection because there are some wonderful dog / human relationships, but once in a lifetime there is a special connection, one that you never expected or looked for. It is, I suppose, not that different from finding the right partner in life, something I have never had the good fortune to do. I have had two wives, and sadly I was never able to be what they wanted me to be. Either Lottie didn't want me to be anything in particular (which seems likely since she is a dog and what would she know?) or serendipitously I was the right person at the right time for her. If someone could tell me she eventually forgot about me, that would be a great relief, but I don't suppose anyone can know that. From time to time I fantasise about going to see her, but I know that would be a terrible mistake, for me and for her, and it would serve no purpose.

If I ever have another dog, will I make the mistake of thinking she is Lottie? I don't think so. When you have your second child, you might make the mistake of thinking they are going to be a clone of the first one but of course they aren't. My next dog, if there is one, won't be Lottie or anything like her. She will, though, probably be an Airedale Terrier, the dog we didn't get when we got Lottie. That's a paradox, isn't it? I didn't want to get a dog at all, and if we were going to I wanted an Airedale, but in either of those circumstances I would not have met Lottie. They say it is better to have loved and lost than not to have loved at all, but I'm not sure they have got that right.

This might all be sentimental tosh, so let's go back to the grooming thing. With the long-haired Manchester Terrier I had many years ago I always thought there ought to be something I could do with the fur she shed, but Lottie had even more and Liz came up with an excellent answer. She put it out in the garden for the birds to take for nesting material, and to my surprise they really did. As fast as she hung it up in the trees it disappeared. I should think it made a very comfortable nest, and I rather liked the idea. I have never been attracted to short-haired dogs (I know, I said I love dogs, but by now you might be wondering if that is quite right, on account of the number of dogs I don't like – small ones, short-haired ones, three-legged ones, for example), but suffice it to say it is long-haired dogs I find most attractive. Being a very tactile person, there is something for me in a dog's coat you can get your hands into ..... anyway, enough of that, except that perhaps I do have an excuse. The domestic dog is a direct descendent of the wolf, and wolves have long coats. Well, that is my excuse and I'm sticking to it. Would I have loved Lottie if she had had a short coat? I have no idea. Perhaps, but also perhaps not as much. I probably wouldn't have picked her if she hadn't been what she was (the picture on the back cover of this book is the image we fell in love with), but on the other hand would I have been given a say in the matter? Like any other what if, that is unknowable.

29

Fear

We could have known, had we understood more, that very first day, when they brought Lottie to us and she shivered with fear in our living room, that fear was going to be her all-pervasive emotion, the thing that made her life difficult for her, and the thing we had to devote ourselves to helping her overcome, for a long time to come, perhaps for the rest of her life.

I don't know but I don't imagine dogs, or any other animals, fear the unknown. We humans do, because we have brains large enough, and developed enough, to ponder the imponderable. It's why humans have religion and the other animals don't, but don't get me started on that subject. Lottie showed us very clearly that her fear came from her experience. One of my fears is of the dentist, and that is also based on experience. In that instance what I am afraid of is what I have experienced, so it is not a phobia, which is an irrational fear, it is a rational fear. The difference between my fear of the dentist and Lottie's fear, for example of other dogs, is that I can rationalise that when I get out of the dentist's practice whatever bad things happened in there they are over. Until the next time, anyway. A dog has no ability to rationalise, or to project. Well, perhaps they can to some extent. I should think a dog that has been beaten will always fear the person who did that every time they see them. And in some cases I should think they will come to fear everyone, because everyone is a human with the potential to hurt them.

In Lottie's case, we realised early on that the humans she feared were men. We could only assume the people who had caught her and caged her were men, which seems very likely, and we could also only assume that was done with a certain amount of brutality. The immediate problem here was that I am, you probably realise, a man. I was the person who needed to get physically the closest to Lottie, if for no other reason than that I had, at various stages of her development, to carry her out to the garden or the car or into the vet. So what I had to do was to prove to her that not all men are the same. I had had that very problem with Liz as it happened, but in the event it turned out to be easier to persuade Lottie that all men are not the same than it did with Liz. It seems that for the brain power we humans have, sometimes what we call a dumb animal has more ability to learn than we do.

And Lottie did learn not to be afraid of me. She flinched whenever I wielded anything that might reasonably be something to beat her with, like an umbrella, so I had to learn not to do that. To think about what might be seen by her as a weapon. To think like she did, and that's interesting because one can try to think like a dog but in that situation the one who taught me to think like her was of course Lottie herself. By responding to how she responded to me, I learned to be the person she needed me to be. It was not only a very rewarding thing to achieve, it gave me an insight not only into Lottie's mind but into the mind of dogs generally. I am no expert and I have never trained in dog psychology, but I venture to suggest that Lottie taught me something I didn't even know I needed to know. Am I going to try to explain what that was? No, I'm afraid I am not. I couldn't even try. I recently watched the film Born Free. You may remember it. Joy Adamson developed a very special relationship with the lion cub, Elsa, based not on any soft-hearted notion of animals, which surely would not have worked with an animal born to be wild, but instead on the reality of what she and the lion taught each other. As a result, she came to love Elsa.

It may be presumptuous, even impertinent, to suggest that some owners treat their dogs more like toys than sentient beings, and I'm sorry but you can't have a relationship with a toy.

Anyway, back to the story. Lottie's fear was not something to try to knock out of her, and neither was it something to get irritated about or frustrated at. It was something to understand. I understood why she was afraid of men, and together we overcame that fear, so the next step was to start working on her other fears. We were working on her fear of getting out of the car, and that was done in baby steps. One of those steps showed great promise.

We took her to the place on the Downs where she was used to getting out of the car, albeit tentatively, and then we drove home, but as we approached the house I asked Liz to stop the car, just a few doors away. We could tell that Lottie recognised where we were. She had developed a way of relaxing as we got near the house, and sniffing at the open window to pick up a scent she recognised, and this gave me a clue to the next stage. We were close enough to the house that when Liz stopped and I got out, it didn't occur to Lottie that we weren't actually quite there. She happily got out, as usual, and all she had to do was trot for a few seconds and there she was, on our front path.

All we had to do then, each time we drove home, was to stop the car a little further back, get her out and let her trot home. She pulled a little, obviously keen to get there, but that didn't matter. In fact that told us how she was progressing, because as she pulled less we knew it was time to stop the car just a little further back, that she was feeling less stressed about it. And before long I was able to walk her right from the end of the road. As time went by and we no longer had to do this, we would think back to those baby steps and marvel that they worked, but also how far she had come since then, because we hadn't had to do it for a long time.

Far and away Lottie's greatest fear was of other dogs. I can only think this came from being locked in a pound, when she was very young and untutored in the way dog packs work, with hundreds of other dogs, in Romania. Many of those dogs would themselves have been fearful, and they would have expressed that fear as aggression. The very thought of my Lottie in the midst of a pack of aggressive dogs, perhaps looking for the mother she was never going to see again, is almost unbearable. We know she was very young when she was captured – she was only eight months old when we got her. I don't know how they knew how old she was, but I suppose as she had some veterinary treatment the vet would perhaps have certified that. A dog that is thrown on its own resources will learn to fend for itself, but such a young dog would surely have been overwhelmed in that environment. Were there fights? I should think that's very likely. Did the staff stop the fights? That I cannot know. I'm sorry if I inadvertently cast aspersions on Romania, but I'm pretty sure it is safe to assume that stray dogs there are not cared for as we here know the RSPCA and Dogs Trust care for them. These charities in the UK are very well funded by the huge number of people who care about animal welfare, and they are staffed by people who, I am sure, do their jobs for the love of the animals they rescue. Romania is not a rich country, and if the state of their orphanages at the end of the Communist era is anything to go by it seems safe to guess that people who can treat children that way can surely treat animals at least as badly. Look, I could be wrong, and things could really have changed, and if you know better do please get in touch and let me know. My email address is at the back of this book for such a purpose.

So, by the time Lottie arrived in Hove, on top of all the stress and anxiety of the journey, let alone in a van with a lot of other dogs, it is hardly surprising that she carried with her an abiding fear of dogs. Luckily, since she wouldn't leave our living room for some time, and then she only went as far as the back garden, there was at least a considerable period when she was not going to have to face any other dog.

I haven't seen her for two years, and I understand from the reports I have had that she has made considerable progress, but I should say that at the time I left her this was still an ongoing project. And this is how it all happened.

It started with a dog expert who really was an expert. Not only did he know about dogs, but he had a deep love for them. Actually, I'll just fill you in with what happened before we met him, so you have the full picture, and you can see the miracle he worked.

Once we got Lottie walking on the Downs, it was inevitable that she was going to come across other dogs. Not only is it an obvious place for Brightonians to walk their dogs but it's also where professional dog walkers go. I have never quite seen the point of having a dog and paying someone else to walk it, but perhaps I shouldn't be too judgmental (I know, I am); there must be many people who find this a workable compromise, having a dog but having to be out all day at work, and someone else taking the dog during the day is, I suppose, better than leaving the animal at home alone all day.

The odd dog was something Lottie could avoid. She would scuttle off into the nearest bushes and follow us from her hiding place until the path ahead was clear. When she first did this we worried, but she proved very good at knowing where we were even when we didn't know where she was.

The bigger problem was the dog walkers with their packs, often of anything up to a dozen dogs. This was way more than Lottie could handle. Fortunately, these packs are fairly well established groups. They meet each other on a daily basis so they behave as a pack, and dogs outside the pack are not necessarily very interesting. That didn't stop one or two trying to find Lottie, but failing that they were more interested in rejoining their pack. In fairness to the walkers, they tended to behave responsibly, and when they could see that Lottie was afraid they tended to take charge of their charges.

The logical next step, so Liz said, was to enrol Lottie in a pack. That sounded pretty improbable to me. Her overwhelming imperative was to avoid any group of dogs she spotted, so how were we ever going to get her to join one? And why? Well, I suppose the answer to why was that if we could get her into a pack she would overcome her fear of other dogs. But hold on, her fear of dogs was the reason why she would not be able to join a pack, so this was kind of a circular idea. A chicken and egg situation, in which Lottie was chicken.

And this was when Richard came to the rescue. He was a dog walker, but one with a difference. He walked troubled dogs, helping them to relate to him and other dogs, including several which were his own, so he always knew which he could put with any troubled dog he was given to work with. I wasn't convinced about this, but it wasn't my decision, and whilst I might have given the impression that Liz made the decisions (which was true) I should add that her decisions did tend to be good ones. I didn't like the way she made them, but I couldn't often argue with the results.

The first step was to accustom Lottie to just being near the pack, so Richard walked with, say, half a dozen dogs, while Liz walked, with Lottie on the training lead, quite a way behind. Would she accept the distance and not worry about the other dogs? Well, she did and she didn't, because one thing we knew about her was that she wasn't consistent. We would think we had achieved a small victory, only to find the next day or the next week that we remembered how she did it, whatever it was, but that didn't mean she did. Repetition is obviously the key to learning anything, whether it involves a dog or a child, or come to that an adult. And dogs have a shorter memory than humans have, or grown-up humans anyway, so you have not only to repeat any given lesson but you have to do it regularly, before the animal has a chance to forget what it has learned.

Nevertheless, Lottie did learn to walk behind the pack without too much worry, so moving on from there was simply a matter of Liz walking a little closer to the pack each time. Sometimes Lottie would accept this and sometimes she wouldn't. I should like to say this was something to do with the above, the thing about having a short memory, but I think it also has to be said that Lottie has moods. I won't say that has anything to with her being female. She is, for whatever reason, a moody dog. Sometimes she wanted to be with us, and other times she wanted to be left alone. Sometimes she was happy, as far as we could tell, and sometimes she was sad. At least she appeared sad. Was it something we had said? No, surely not. Her moods, I can be pretty sure, had nothing to do with us. I can only think they were a hangover from her past life. Sometimes she has what Winston Churchill called 'black dog' moments, only in her case they were more black and tan dog moments. If she were a human she would perhaps be diagnosed with clinical depression and prescribed some nasty drug she would become dependent on for the rest of her life, but thankfully she is a dog, not a human, and also thankfully neither Liz nor I would never do such a thing to a human, let alone a dog.

So if she was on one of these walks, following Richard and his pack, and she decided this was not a good day, there would be little choice but either to walk her elsewhere or give up entirely and take her home. We had learned how far she could be pushed, whatever it was we wanted her to do. Encouragement, even strong encouragement, was one thing (that might actually be two things), but forcing her was only ever going to be counter productive. It could only make her more fearful, and in any case it was also likely to damage her trust in us. We had promised her, when we first got her, that we were never going to hurt her, and that was a promise that was not hard to keep. Yes, I know, she didn't know we had made that promise. On the other hand, you never know, perhaps she did. Actually, she couldn't know what we meant when we said it, but she learned what we meant by our actions. In short, she learned to trust us.

This was rather like she learned to trust me, that even though I am a man I was never going to beat her, and the only way she could learn that was that of course I never did beat her. I never threatened her either. I did what she needed, not what I needed. Here I am going to ask that rhetorical question again, the one about whether we indulged her too much. The answer to that, categorically, is no. I am a great believer in discipline (more for myself than others), and I also know that dogs, being pack animals, must have discipline in order to understand their position in the pack. Lottie never tried to be the leader of the pack, because we never allowed her to think for a moment about such a thing. But being the leader is about, among all the other things, compassion and understanding. Liz and I did not always take the same view of her training and rehabilitation, but neither did either of us ever think the answer was to show less compassion for fear that she might take advantage. We didn't, and she rewarded us by not taking advantage. Lottie is a good girl.

Actually, and here I am going out on a limb because this is just a feeling, but I suspect it never occurred to Lottie to try to establish herself as the pack leader. Whether that is because in human terms she is just too nice, or because she was so downtrodden when she came to us she didn't have that instinct, I don't know. There was much she didn't know about being a dog, perhaps because in the wild dogs are taught their place in the pack they are born into, and even in their relationship with humans they are taught the same thing (which is that they are never the leader), and she had of course not had either of those experiences. In that respect we had an advantage, I suppose, because she was a clean slate, a dog we could create in any image we chose. What we wanted was for her to be more dog than she was, and I think what we meant by that was that she should learn to enjoy being a dog, both in the company of humans and in the company of other dogs.

30

Lottie Becomes a Pack Animal

What Richard gave her was the latter. Gradually, very gradually, she learned to connect with other dogs. Somewhere deep in the recesses of her mind was the instinct to connect to dogs. Perhaps what Richard gave her in fact was the very thing I have been talking about, a place in the pack. And it wasn't him on his own, because he trusted his dogs to ease Lottie into the group. At first, they tended to overwhelm her, and she would simply run away, but any dog will soon lose interest if the object of its attentions doesn't respond. They are not so different from humans in that respect. His dogs tried to play with her, and since she made it very clear she wasn't going to do that they went back to playing with each other. That, in fact, was what she needed. They had made a connection, which she had rejected, but it enabled her to figure them out. Making that connection, or at least trying to, gave Lottie information, the information she needed to size them up.

Another issue for Lottie was that she didn't understand play. Again, I can only wonder why. Was it because of her genetic inheritance as a working dog? A shepherd dog has better things to do than play. Or was it that she hadn't played with any siblings in her litter? We cannot know if that was what happened of course, but if it was it would explain why she hadn't learned the benefit of play. Actually, here I am going to digress very slightly and wonder if it is not only working dogs that are less interested in play than is normal. What I mean by normal is what I have said more than once, and I make no apology for iterating it when necessary. Dogs are domesticated wild animals. Why would they want to play? Wolves don't play. They do as pups, but that is necessary because they learn through play. Once they are grown, though, and have the responsibility to find food and all the other things they might need to do depending on their status in the pack, play is irrelevant. So why do pet dogs play, even as adults? Why do most dogs play all of their lives? Well, correct me if I'm wrong, but on reflection I shall frame this as a question rather than a statement, so you can't, but do dogs play because they are infantilised by their owners, and used by their owners as toys? Do they play to entertain because that is what their owners want them to do so it's what they teach them and encourage them to do? Throwing a ball for a dog to fetch might connect with its primeval instinct to catch prey, but not ad infinitem ad nauseam in the park.

There were two reasons why we never had Lottie run after a ball. The first was because even though we tried she didn't respond. We couldn't teach her to play in that way. She just wasn't interested, so that was fine. The other was that once we understood that she didn't want to do it we learned there was a sound reason why she didn't. She was not a toy, and we didn't want her to be one. We used to worry about her being what we thought was a bit morose, but that was anthropomorphising. She probably wasn't morose, she was not being more dog in the sense of the stuff I've just been talking about, doing what humans want in part to entertain, she was being more dog in the way her genes told her to be, and a lot of that was simply not connecting with humans and not doing what they wanted.

What she got from Richard's dogs was, I think, what she should have had as a puppy. Don't run away with the idea that when she did learn to play she did much of it. If a dog chased her and she cottoned on to the fact that this was a game, she would run away, and then the other dog would turn and run from her, and sometimes she understood that and sometimes she didn't. On the occasions when she did, she would give chase in turn and it became a proper game. It never lasted though; Lottie is not a fast runner. She just isn't built for it. On one occasion she chased a lurcher into a sand bunker on the golf course and for a moment they both thought that was fun, but whereas the lurcher liked it so he wanted to do more, Lottie decided she had done that briefly, and, well, that was enough. Some of Richard's dogs did manage to engage her in play, but it was never for very long. Still, it was tremendous progress, and we just loved to see her having fun with her own kind, something we thought she was never going to do. It gave us a brief window on what she was thinking, that fun is good. Albeit momentarily she was happy, so we were happy.

In all the time I spent with Lottie, I never once heard her snarl or growl at another dog. She would run and hide from them, she would ignore them, but what she would never do is be aggressive with them. Perhaps she has an underdog mentality, which would hardly be surprising, but perhaps if she did she would growl at them, so perhaps that is not relevant. I would also have to take into account, I suppose, that she was never exposed to an aggressive dog. She only kept polite company, and in any case I'm quite sure that if she did meet an aggressive dog she would just turn tail and run. This is where her genes are betrayed by her experience. She was bred to fend off wolves and bears, to stand her ground, to avoid actual physical combat if possible, because after all a Carpathian Shepherd is not a match for a wolf if it comes to actual fighting. Wolves hunt in packs, and as far as I know Romanian sheep farmers put two or three dogs with the herd, so the dogs also work as a team. Lottie had of course never been in a team of Carpathian Shepherds, and in any case she is not pure-bred, so perhaps her excuse is she is let down by the breeding of the dog her mother or father had the dalliance with. But also perhaps she never grew into a brave dog because of her sorry start in life.

Richard's dogs seemed to know, don't ask me how, not to harass Lottie, so when she did start to socialise with them it was on her own terms. Everything is done on Lottie's own terms in any case, but it helped that under Richard's tutelage what Lottie had not had as a pup she got, at least to some extent, now. His dogs didn't have a pack leader because he was their pack leader, so there was never any competition for top dog place. They all knew their place, and Lottie came to know hers. And that, I think, was what she needed in order to build her confidence. I don't think she ever saw me as the leader of her pack. Perhaps this was because I never tried to be, notwithstanding the advice I had read to establish that relationship with your dog, but also perhaps because I spoiled my chance of being her leader from the beginning, by treating her as an equal. When we played rough games, perhaps she saw me as another pup in her litter rather than a parent figure teaching her how a dog behaves. I don't know this, of course, and if you are a dog professional you might think this is foolish, but hey, she was my dog, and this is my book, and that's what I think.

Gradually, when she was taken to meet Richard she got used to his dogs running up and greeting her, which they always did. It was obvious that they had absorbed her into the pack. Note that they greeted her, she didn't greet them. Lottie will never be like that, you know, easy going. Like some women I have known, she never makes the first move. She reacts but she doesn't initiate. Well, that's fine. I could say it's because she does everything on her own terms, but I suspect it is more that she will always wait to hear what the other dog has to say before deciding if it's safe to connect. That's actually probably not that different from any normal dog, it's just more finely honed in her. She came to feel safe with Richard's pack, even though the group varied most days because he had clients whose dogs were included on his walks at different times of the week. But because the core pack was safe Lottie could handle the part-time pack members. I don't know how to express the feeling we got from seeing her being more dog, as we called it, more normal as other people might say. I can only tell you it was hugely satisfying. We wanted her to be happy, and that would surely come from just being like any normal dog, doing what normal dogs do. I mentioned much earlier that dogs don't have a lot of demands on them, other than silly owners making them do tricks, and we wanted Lottie to have that kind of life. A dog's life.

Another reason why it was good that she accepted the pack was that it made her less dependent on us. We didn't mind her being dependent on us, far from it, we just knew it wasn't good for her. Like a child growing up and finding their way in the world through new relationships, we knew Lottie needed to find her way in the world through the relationship she might have with her own kind. The relationship between dog and human is something good that has developed over thousands of years and is now hard-wired into all modern dogs, but their relationship with each other is in some ways at least as important, because genetically it pre-dates their connection to humans. And what Richard's pack taught Lottie was something we couldn't teach her. We could tell her, for want of a better way of putting it, what she needed to do, but only other dogs could show her what she should be doing. For this reason she developed faster with the pack than we had been able to move her forward. That was only natural and I had no complaints about it.

But there was another benefit to Lottie developing dog friendships as well. It helped her to be less afraid of all dogs. Once she understood that not every dog was a threat, she started to make judgments about each dog that she met, in a way she had not been able to before.

This meant that in due course, in the rec for her late evening walk, if she met a dog she fancied playing with she would do the things dogs do with other dogs to let them know they are up for a game. More often than not, though, the other dog's owner didn't want theirs to play, they wanted it to play with them, to chase a ball or just walk with them. They would even put them on the lead to make sure they didn't play. We found this was very common, that a lot of dog owners just did not want their dog to play with other dogs. It was nothing to do with

Lottie, it was clearly that they saw their dog as belonging to them, that their dog should have human relationships, not dog ones. I always found that not only frustrating for Lottie, who wasn't allowed to play with them, but for the dogs themselves, because connecting with other dogs is what they wanted and what they needed, but were not allowed to do by owners who thought of them as possessions, not animals with animal instincts.

And then one day Lottie met her match. When I say her match, I don't mean it like it sounds. She met a St Bernard called Kipling. Kipling was two things Lottie liked; he was big (she has always preferred big dogs) and he was male (I don't know why but she has always preferred male dogs too). Most importantly he had some innate sensitivity that made him friendly but not pushy. He knew, in short, how to handle a woman. When we met Kipling and his owner on a walk we knew we could let the two of them go off and have fun (no, not that kind of fun; Kipling had been 'done', and our Lottie was a good girl). We did wonder what sort of puppies they would make. Beautiful ones, and big ones too. All right, I have to say it: Lottie and Kipling would have made exceedingly good puppies.

I have sometimes thought that Lottie would have lovely pups and it's a shame she would never be able to do that, but the world doesn't need more unwanted dogs. At the time of writing people are paying silly money for dogs that don't even have a pedigree, on the basis, as far as I can see, that they don't shed their fur. I'm sorry but that seems to me to be a strange criterion for choosing a pet. I mean, goldfish don't shed fur, and you don't have to take them for walks or house train them and you don't have to feed them with expensive meat, but we live in strange times, so I'll drop that subject right now.

For the first two years after I left Lottie I got regular reports from Liz about her progress. That contact has gone now, so there are no more reports, but I'm pretty sure that Lottie has continued to progress, to be more dog, and to enjoy life. She deserves to enjoy life. Well, don't all dogs?

31

Crow and Dog Scarers

Another fear Lottie had was crow scarers. I don't actually know how these devices work, but they are used by farmers to, well obviously, scare crows off. They sound to me much like shotguns. For all I know perhaps they are. The point is they are loud and you never know, if you are walking across the Downs, where they are situated. Most people would not perhaps even notice them once they got used to them, but Lottie really hated them. They completely spooked her. We would be walking along quite happily and they they would go off, always several of them a few seconds apart. And Lottie became uncontrollable. She never lost her sense of direction, so she always knew where the car had been parked, and she turned and ran for it. It was impossible to catch her, and calling her was a completely pointless exercise, not that she had much recall at the best of times.

When she was frightened in that way she lost any possible communication with us. People who think you can always coax a dog with food would have been standing there holding a treat, looking foolish as Lottie disappeared into the distance. At first it was really dispiriting. We were sad for her, because I would have to describe her fear as terror, and we were also saddened that we were unable to communicate with her in that state. For those minutes, she wasn't our dog. She was in survival mode and there was nothing else. There was of course no choice but to follow her. If you are a dog trainer and you are thinking we should have left her to get on with it, that she would have learned to come back to us, you haven't been paying attention. No, she would not. She would have found the car (or any car, since she wasn't good at recognising either of ours) and stood by it until we appeared. Even worse, if any roads had to be crossed she would have been in great danger. During the crow-scaring season, there was often no choice but to keep her on the training lead, and then when they went off at least we could let her lead us back to the car under slightly less panicky circumstances, and minus the fear that she might get lost or run over.

One good piece of advice we were given was not to try to calm her down when this happened. You wouldn't necessarily think of this but to try to calm her, we were told, would confirm in her mind that there was something to be afraid of. I will readily admit that the dog specialists we learned from did come up with good advice, things we could not have known ourselves. Teaching Lottie to be more normal was therefore a mix of their good advice about things we didn't know, and our own instincts and our love for her. Dog trainers did not necessarily think our instincts were worth much against their knowledge, and I suspect they also didn't think our love was good for her, that it was imposing human feelings on her. Well, we understood her and we knew that we didn't love her too much.

In time she did actually learn to take the crow scarers (and clay pigeon shooting) more in her stride. The first time we heard the bang and watched her reaction, and she hesitated and thought it through but she didn't run, was a huge relief. I know police dogs (and horses) have to be trained not to bolt when they hear loud noises, and my understanding is that the only way they can learn this is to be exposed to them, that eventually they learn that the noise is horrible (and there I would agree with them) but that it doesn't represent a danger. All animals, and humans come to that, can be acclimatised to things that feel threatening to the extent that they are no longer threatening. My own experience was, many years ago, as a reserve soldier in the Army. It took me a while to stop being affected by loud bangs, which are an occupational hazard in that line of work.

We despaired for a while that we might have to stop walking Lottie near farmland, but thankfully it did sort of get resolved. It's much like life generally; you think you will never resolve some problem but then you do. In my experience, the problems you think you can do nothing about tend to stop being problems of their own accord. For this reason, it paid us not to angst too much about Lottie's problems. The fact is she resolved most of them without us particularly being involved. Having said that, I need to add that the reason she resolved them was surely because we gave her a safe space in which to do that. That, on reflection, might well have been the best thing we ever did for her, to give her the security from which to face the world.

Is that any different from what we do as parents for our children? It begs the question: is there as big a difference between the psychology of dogs and humans as we think, or should I say as we like to think? Dogs and humans have shared their lives for so many thousands of years, is it beyond the realms of possibility that we share more, psychologically, than we think, or than we understand, or even than we are prepared to believe? We have shared experiences over many many generations, so is it possible that in our own way we have actually come to share the way we think? Yes, I know, it's all quite fanciful, but there is just one issue that makes me question the veracity of that belief, that it is too fanciful. The way we think is expressed in words, to each other but also to ourselves. Dogs don't have words, well, not in the way we do. Our ability to communicate is so much more sophisticated than theirs that we cannot imagine they are thinking anything like us, but what if dogs had words? If they could express thoughts in a way we understand, would it turn out that they have thoughts not that dissimilar from ours, after millennia of a shared existence?

Is, therefore, the relationship between humans and dogs restricted by nothing more than our perceived superiority, because we have language, and we can communicate not just things (because after all a dog can bark, which will tell other dogs something) but also we can communicate ideas and concepts and thoughts and fears and hopes, all things that are denied dogs, and of course all the other animals.

However, as I say, this is all very fanciful, so if you think I am rambling you are welcome to ignore all of it. Or not.

My point (yes, I do actually have a point), is that Lottie was trapped in a dog world which we couldn't enter, and she couldn't enter ours, but was it a mistake to believe that those worlds must remain entirely separate? Which leads me to this conclusion, if a question can be a conclusion – were we communicating with Lottie more than we thought we were?

A child cannot easily express its fear, let's say of the dark, because it doesn't have the necessary sophisticated language needed to describe complex feelings. A dog doesn't have even the limited ability of a small child, but what would it tell us if it had our ability to communicate ideas? When I looked at Lottie, I didn't see a dumb animal, I saw a brain developed over thousands of years in a relationship with humans, learning to do what humans want, learning to want the company of humans, not so very different, therefore, from humans, but lacking that one thing that humans have, the ability to communicate their thoughts. Or in Lottie's case, their fears.

Which brings me full circle, because Lottie could not know that repeated exposure to what she feared, whether it was other dogs or cows or crow scarers, would help her to come to terms with those scary things. The only reason we knew it was not because we have more innate intelligence but because we could read what other people said on the subject. We might think we were terribly clever because we figured out that exposure would get Lottie used to loud bangs, but that idea didn't pop into our head unbidden, it came from exposure to ideas, not all of which were relevant but which combined led us to the answer.

Am I saying humans are more intelligent than dogs? No, because it is a completely invalid concept. It is not comparing like with like. The IQ test for becoming a member of Mensa includes questions that in my opinion do not measure intelligence at all (no, that is not sour grapes because I failed the test, because I didn't). They measure one's ability to understand what someone else means when they ask a question. Cryptic crosswords, which many people find unfathomable, don't depend on the solver being clever, they depend on them understanding what the setter is talking about, and that can be learned. In my humble opinion (yes, I can do humility), a good relationship between a human and a dog is formed not because the dog is a clever one, but because for whatever reason the person and the dog get each other.

I may have mentioned this before, but I am a hopeless judge of character, but that involves humans. I cannot say whether Lottie got me, but I can say that I got her. OK, I can say that I believe I got her, and that will have to do. It is also, unfortunately, what made it so hard to leave her.

In this chapter, I may have inadvertently given the impression I know what I'm talking about, for which I apologise. In my day job, as the director of a small, specialised medical foundation, which includes writing on health issues, I really do know what I'm talking about. However, in my health writing my approach is not to claim to know the answers but to know which questions to ask. If I know anything about anything it is that too often experts are quite good at coming up with answers but less good, a lot less good, at asking the right questions. In my field of healthcare, they usually ask the question that will produce the answer they are looking for, because that's the answer that makes a profit for someone. I mention this merely as my excuse for writing this chapter, in the hope that you will get my point, which is to wonder, publicly, about Lottie's psychology, and of course by extension the psychology of all dogs.

I have no pecuniary interest in canine medicine, and I write as an amateur, but it is just possible that that's the way to ask the questions that have answers that improve the lives, in this case, of dogs. I had no thought, when with Liz I took Lottie on, of becoming involved in issues that were always going to be beyond my ken. What I write is one man's thoughts on this subject. Lottie will always be beyond the reach of anyone to understand what goes on in her head, but is she actually much different from any other dog in that respect? How much do we actually know about what any animal is thinking? Look, as far as I can see human psychology is based as much on guesswork as science, and that involves people who speak the same language as us, so what chance do we have with animals that don't?

If you can bear my musing yet further, I wonder how much we assume about our pets, anthropomorphising, inevitably, because we are human and the human condition is actually the only one we have any understanding of. So when a dog misbehaves, for example, we are surprised, as if she should know better, or even because we've told her about that before. Hence Liz's disappointment that Lottie wouldn't rush to greet her when she came into the house. Why should she? Well, in fairness, Liz would say she should because that's what other dogs do, that it's normal dog behaviour. Is it, or is my Lottie the only dog that actually knows that rushing to greet its owner when they come home is in fact nothing more than the behaviour humans have taught dogs, that it's not normal for a dog at all? Do we humans create dogs in our own image, because frankly we don't have the intelligence to see them for what they are? We constantly get our relations with other humans wrong, and they are like us and we should understand them. What chance do we have with our dogs?

And all of this is the reason I didn't mind Lottie not coming and wagging her tail at me. Why, against Liz's instructions, I went to say hello to her. Of course, it is just possible that that is not normal behaviour for a human. I'm not going to argue with you on that one.

32

Two Vets Lottie

For all her psychological problems when she came to England, Lottie inevitably had more than her fair share of physiological problems too. It would have been surprising if she hadn't. We don't know the circumstances of her very early life, but at some point as a puppy she was caught and taken to a large pound for stray dogs. There, she would have been put on a bad diet and she would have been under enormous stress, which as well as affecting her mind seriously impacted on her body. And then, before she was transported from Romania to Britain she had the rabies vaccine, and that had weakened her immune system. All of that, combined with the poor diet, would have killed a lesser dog, as probably would the distemper, so strange as it seemed to us we actually had adopted a dog with a strong constitution. If we could find the right answers to her immediate problems, that was going to help her to survive and thrive, and she did both.

For a few weeks it was quite impossible for her to see a vet. We could hardly get near her ourselves, let alone take her to yet another strange place where yet another strange person was going to handle her. Before too long, thankfully, we were at last able to take her to the local allopathic vet. I had to carry her to the car, and from the car into the practice, but she let me. She always let me carry her, which was both helpful and a relief, because it meant she was starting to trust me. Either that or she was too frightened to fight me, but I think not. Well, I like to think not.

What came out of that visit was that the vet was able to tell us there was nothing wrong with her legs. Her problem with walking in our presence was in her brain, but of course in those early weeks when she spent all her time in our living room she walked, because she ate her food and she used the toilet, so I suppose on reflection we must have known that.

Anyway, it wasn't the primary reason for the consultation. When she came to us she had a large ugly growth on her lower lip, but that was a reaction to the rabies vaccine and Liz had dealt very well with that. The big problem was a large hot spot on her side, which she nibbled endlessly. It clearly troubled her greatly, and if it distressed her it distressed us too. The allopathic vet had little to offer for this, which he diagnosed as more psychological in origin than physiological, so then we took her to the homeopathic vet, who was likely to be in a better position to help with a problem that was both physical and emotional. It took months for this to heal, but it did heal and that was a relief, as much to us as to Lottie.

If you are reading the paperback version of this book, you will be able to see in the photo on the back cover that Lottie once had a full-length tail. It occurred to us that that picture, taken in the dog pound in Romania, might not actually be the dog we now had, but we didn't think so. We got to know Lottie, and we could see it was her. We never found out what happened to the other half, but as with the distemper she presumably had good veterinary attention because that at least never caused her a problem. Fair enough, she didn't wag it, but that had nothing to do with its physical shortcomings, that was because she just isn't a waggy dog. At first, we felt sorry for her loss, but as we came to know and love her we accepted it as part of her charm. (Yes, I know what you're thinking, that the owner of a dog with only three legs would love it despite the loss, or even because of it, but we've discussed that so let's not go there.)

Another problem Lottie had, and still has as far as I know, is that she was an itchy dog. Itchy dogs are a well recognised problem, and looking online we found any number of products which promised to resolve the problem, but here I must refer you to my personal view of healthcare, which remember was my day job for many years. My biggest single issue with medical practice is that it is quite good at coming up with answers but it is a lot less good at asking questions, and not infrequently the answers might be quite good ones except that they are not actually answers because you cannot solve a problem if you don't know what the problem is. This applies, naturally, to veterinary medicine just as much as it does to human medicine, with the added complication that a doctor can ask the patient about their symptoms but a vet can only ask the animal's owner those questions, and that's less helpful.

Liz takes a different view of all this, and she ordered

one of the wonder products after another, all of which, surprisingly, proved not to be wonder products after all.

I know what you're thinking, that this was just fleas, because they are the first thing you would think of with itching, but Lottie did not appear to have fleas. The vet confirmed this after a thorough examination of her coat. Later on, she did have the odd flea, because once Lulu came to us she was prone to them and inevitably she passed them to Lottie. Strangely, though, fleas don't seem to like Lottie, and every time the itching flared up Liz gave her another flea treatment but to be honest it wasn't the solution because fleas weren't the problem.

Before she was spayed (Lottie, not Liz), a pattern started to emerge about the itching. It flared up each time she came into season, which seemed a perfectly reasonable explanation, even if it didn't necessarily give us a solution, other than that we knew it was likely to lessen after the season finished. Strangely, though, after she was spayed she did occasionally have a flare-up of the itching, and this led me to wonder if she wasn't prone to phantom seasons. I don't know if there is such a thing as phantom seasons, but trust me, if there isn't that would not necessarily be a reason for Lottie not to have them.

Meanwhile, she had to suffer the indignity of showering with Liz, covered with obnoxious-smelling shampoos guaranteed to solve the problem, and maybe they did help a little. She would always go straight out into the garden and dig herself a hole in the earth to sleep in, and for all I know it was something in the soil that helped as much as or more than the shampoo.

Just as Lottie overcame most of her emotional difficulties through our love and attention, she grew in health and strength through something that in my work in human health I believe to be the single most important element to the maintenance of good health, and that is good nutrition. I have always been shocked and disappointed by the medical profession's grudging acceptance that what we eat 'might affect our health'. Isn't it interesting, though, that dog food, especially the more expensive kind, always boasts that it has been formulated by experts in canine nutrition? When did you ever see food for people that has been formulated by experts in human nutrition? Does that mean dogs are more important or that vets know more about how essential good nutrition is for health than doctors do? Of course it might be neither of those. It might simply be that pet-food companies know how to sell their product. Mind you, that still doesn't explain why we are so cavalier about human nutrition. Why don't the manufacturers of food for people sell it on the basis of its nutritional value just like dog-food manufacturers do? I have to say, the whole thing is puzzling.

Back to Lottie though. We didn't know what she had been fed before we got her, but it was reasonable to assume it was kibble of some kind. Now, I didn't have a strong opinion about kibble, not knowing anything about it, and I'm not one for formulating opinions on things I know little or nothing about, but for Liz it is the work of the devil (she's a rather black and white person; things are either good or bad, and if they are bad they are probably his work). Once Liz put me straight about kibble, I could see that it may have been formulated by experts in canine nutrition but all that tells me is that they say what they are paid to say. Don't get me started on 'experts' though.

The most obvious thing, as far as I can see, is to feed any animal a species-appropriate diet. This applies to humans as well, but I'll stop myself there on that subject. So the question is, what would a dog eat in the wild? Fair enough, a domestic dog that becomes feral will eat almost anything, but I'm not talking about them; I am, I suppose, talking about the ancestor of all domesticated dogs, the wolf. Wolves, I am pretty sure, don't eat kibble. Kibble, and indeed all manufactured dog food, is designed, yes, to be good for dogs, but it is also designed with two other imperatives in mind. It has to be easy to manufacture from the available resources, and it has to be profitable. Pet-food companies are like any other companies (including pharmaceutical companies); they are in business to make a profit. They are not in business to make animals healthy. So what every pet-food company has to come up with is a product that can reasonably justifiably claim to be nutritious, can be mass produced, and will turn a profit. It also, by the way, has to be sellable. In other words, the buyer (I nearly said the consumer, but of course that is the dogs, and they don't make buying decisions) has to believe in it. So it has to be advertised and packaged and priced in such a way as to persuade people to buy it.

What wolves eat is meat. They don't grow vegetables or cereals to make a balanced, expert-formulated diet, they just kill animals and eat them. If you are vegetarian, you may want to skip the next bit, because what Lottie has always been fed by us is meat. Canine teeth, the ones used for tearing meat, are called canine teeth because canines are dogs. Feeding a dog a diet that does not allow it to tear meat cannot possibly be a species-appropriate diet. It is likely to be bad for their digestion and by extension their general health, and it is likely to be bad for their teeth and gums, because their teeth and gums were genetically developed over hundreds of thousands of years before kibble was invented.

It is certainly true that dogs can survive on manufactured food, but do I actually need to point out that there is an epidemic of canine obesity and rotting gums? I would never feed a dog on a vegetarian diet, let alone a vegan one. I've said it before, but if you don't like the idea that dogs eat meat, then don't get a dog, because anything else is imposing your beliefs on them.

OK, now I am going to admit something about Lottie and her raw meat diet. It wasn't a raw meat diet at first. Lottie is a princess. They say put a dog's food down, and if it doesn't like it that is its problem. Well, I can tell you Lottie could go hungry for longer than I could watch her going hungry. What I had to do, to show her how to be more dog, was lightly cook the meat, just flash fry it to take away the rawness of it, and then she would eat it. Then I cooked it less and less, and then I mixed some lightly cooked meat with some raw meat, and in due course she got the hang of it. I love Lottie, but come on, sometimes a dog's got to do what a dog's got to do.

Another thing I find strange (yet another thing) is people who refuse to give their dog bones. Lottie has slightly weakened teeth from the distemper, so we have always been careful about what kind of bones we give her, but the action of chewing bones is important for a dog's dental health. Manufactured dog treats that are supposed to do this are all very well, but they are just a way for pet-food companies to make a profitable product, when bones will do just as well, if not far better. Mind you, Lottie had the bad habit of taking her bones upstairs (if she couldn't take them out into the garden) and chewing them on the carpet, which was not ideal, but what does a little fat and blood on the carpet matter if you love your dog?

33

An Easy Life

It is of course impossible to know what your dog is thinking about you, and we could never know what Lottie was thinking about us, or about anything come to that. It is of course anthropomorphising to think they are thinking anything. Where does instinct end and thinking begin? Lottie didn't actually have to think did she, all she had to do was live from day to day. They live such simple lives, don't they? We of course make it simple for them by providing for them. Lottie had presumably provided for herself as a stray puppy on the streets of Targoviste, which she no longer had to do. Surviving on her own in a harsh if not hostile world was tough, I'm sure, and her life now is easy, but compared with the complexities of the lives we create for ourselves even surviving on the mean streets is really very simple. Hard but simple. No decisions to make, no plans to formulate, no future to plan or worry about. Actually, we humans must be the only animals on Earth who even know what worry is, or come to that what the future is. We ourselves must have been like the other animals, a hundred thousand years ago, when wolves came to live by our camp fires and became dogs. Don't you ever envy them for their simple lives?

One of the things Liz and I had to worry about was of course Lottie herself. She didn't have to worry about herself, and she had no idea we worried about her, but we did all the same. Taking on any dog is a responsibility, more I think than some people realise before they do it (or even after they do it). Were there times when we felt overwhelmed by what we had taken on? Well, we didn't know what we were taking on when we picked her out of a line up, so I think the question now is would we have taken her on if we had known? It's an unanswerable question, but I choose to say yes, we would. Well, I know Liz would, because like most people she is hard-wired to care about the underdog, which I am not. If I have given the impression that I am a caring person willing to sacrifice all if asked to, I may have overstated it. I am in fact pretty hard nosed. You might not like me if you met me. But Lottie accepted me with all my faults, so I would say we suited each other very well. She didn't need anyone who was going to turn to jelly over her. Come to that she didn't actually need anyone. Yes, of course she needed people who were going to take care of her, but what she didn't need was to become dependent on humans. Many dogs do, which I suppose is why they suffer from separation anxiety when left alone in the house. Lottie never did. We know she barked while we were out, because the neighbours complained about it, but that wasn't because she missed us, it was because without us to stop her she was free to stand at the window and bark at every dog that went by. She considered the pavement in front of the house as her territory, and barked at any dog who dared to walk along it. She wasn't protecting our home when she barked, she was protecting her home. We just happened to live there.

In the fantasy world I spend some of my time in, I wonder what it would be like to have a conversation with the dog we live with. Or the cat, although if my extensive experience of cats is anything to go by they would probably look down their nose and dismiss the idea as frivolous. When you have a baby, you have to guess what they want, what they are thinking, and as they grow up you can do that more and more, and then you can ask them. With a dog, though, you are never going to be able to do either of those things, guessing or asking. You are never going to have a conversation with your dog, so your entire relationship, for the whole of their life, is going to be based on what you think they are thinking. In other words, they are going to depend on you guessing what they want. They can learn a few tricks, of course; Lottie knows how to ask to go out into the garden, and she has even learned to tell us when she is hungry, but come on, in human terms they're not very clever tricks are they?

34

You Can Love Them Too Much

Brighton, as you probably know, is by the sea. From time to time there is a story in the Press about someone drowning trying to rescue their dog that has run into the sea in a storm and been swept away. So the question I ask myself is, would I do that? Would I risk my life to save my dog?

Well, first of all, it would never arise, because Lottie has never liked the sea. We took her to the beach to watch other dogs splashing about, running into the water at low tide to fetch a ball (don't get me started again on that one though). Dogs obviously like the sea. But apart from Lottie not wanting to go in the stuff when it was calm, why would she run out into monster waves? Come to that, why does any dog ever do it? If you don't have much experience of these waves, I can tell you they are ridiculously powerful. No-one, even a good swimmer, would have a chance with them. In the kind of stormy sea I'm talking about, you just aren't going to survive being swept out.

So why do owners go in after their dogs? Do they

underestimate the power of the waves? I doubt it. They probably live on the coast, and in any case one look at that kind of sea is more than enough to scare anyone. So do they love their dogs so much that they simply ignore all rational judgment and dive in, regardless? Well, of course, I don't know. All I can say is I wouldn't. As much as I love Lottie, I would not do that. I am simply too rational. You probably think, from all I've said so far, that I'm a softie when it comes to animals. I am, but that has nothing to do with making a rational judgment about risking one's life. In fact diving into a massive sea is not risking one's life, because it is almost a certainty that you are going to die.

Lottie doesn't like water. She avoids puddles, walks carefully round them, so the chance of her going in the sea, even a completely flat one, is, on a scale of one to ten, about nil. Another place we used to take her is the riverside path at Shoreham. It's a nice walk, for us. Other dog walkers use the path, and I'm guessing they do that for the very reason that their dogs like to go in the river. We used to tell Lottie that was what she should be doing but she wasn't easily fooled, she knew better. What other dogs are daft enough to do is of no concern to her. I think Lottie thinks that dogs are strange creatures who don't know much. She is never tempted to do what they are doing, so I have always reckoned she thinks that what they are doing makes no sense, that she is the only dog who knows the correct way to behave. Why any dog would throw itself into the river when there is a perfectly good path that's nice and dry is a mystery to her. Perhaps she imagines they have no sense of direction and end up in the water by mistake. I couldn't say, although on reflection I suppose that is unlikely.

Not long after Lottie came to us, Liz made contact with a woman whose spaniel was, so she said, good at helping stressed dogs to connect, so she was invited to the house to put this spaniel in the garden. I held Lottie in the back doorway while the woman brought her dog in through the back gate. She let it off the lead and it ignored Lottie, ran straight up the garden and fell in the pond. I said to the women, oh look, your dog has fallen in the pond. Oh no, she replied, that's what he does, he loves the water. Well, I don't know who was more puzzled, Lottie or me, but either way it was clear to me that it was my Lottie who was normal and this spaniel who was one dog biscuit short of a snack. If that's normal, I thought, bless Lottie, she's not as strange as I thought. Anyway, so much for this wonder animal being good at dog psychology, because it scrambled out of the pond, ran round the garden a couple of times completely ignoring the dog whose garden it actually was, and then it was time to go home. Lottie and I retired indoors to think about this. Or not.

The more I saw Lottie's reaction to other dogs, the more I started to wonder if in fact she wasn't as strange as we thought. I could see what she was thinking, that she might be the only dog in the world with any sense, but that didn't make her wrong and every other dog right. Apart from the obvious egregious problems she had when she came to us, I started to think she might actually not be as abnormal as we thought. Why should she like swimming? How many Carpathian Shepherds go for a paddle while they are guarding flocks of Romanian sheep? Why should she run around like a demented something on steroids, like a Vizsla of our acquaintance? Why should she run downstairs to greet us, just because every other dog on the planet does that? The question started to arise, exactly what does being more dog really mean? Should we stop worrying that she wasn't doing these things, if she was happy? Did any of it actually matter? If she was happy, we were happy. Actually, that's not exactly right. Liz never stopped worrying that Lottie didn't do all those dog things, could never quite believe that if life was working for Lottie that there was no point worrying about the other stuff.

Having said that, Lottie has made a lot of progress since we parted. Liz found yet another dog expert, one who held outdoor obedience classes, and actually Lottie did well in those, to my surprise. OK, not always. Sometimes she did what the other dogs did, and sometimes she just rolled over on her back and wriggled as if to say no, done enough obedience, let's have some fun, which the other owners found highly amusing, which I expect it was. Luckily, the trainer accepted that Lottie has a limited attention span, and when she says she's done enough there is no point pushing her. I wish I could have been there to see this, but I couldn't. I'm glad she's enjoying her life.

35

Taking a Chance

As every pet owner knows, veterinary treatment is costly, and has become more costly as independent practices have been bought up by large corporations for whom profit understandably comes before the love of animals. For this reason, insuring pets has also become more expensive, because insurance companies are in business for the sole purpose of making a profit.

So how do you choose between insuring your pet or taking a chance that they won't need expensive treatment? Insurance is a form of gambling. The insurance company bets against you in the hope of winning, and they are in the business of winning, like any betting company, so they understand the odds perhaps better than you do.

The sad fact is, though, that every pet will need veterinary care at some time in its life, and those odds get worse as the animal gets older. It's no different from us humans. Now I'm not a great fan of insurance generally, just as I never gamble. I buy insurance where there is no choice, like for my car, and I always take medical cover for travelling abroad, because that is a risk I am prepared to pay an insurance company to cover. I have never insured a pet.

Liz is the opposite, and when we married I added up the money she had paid over the past few years to insure everything from her two cats to the cooker, and the numbers just didn't work, and unusually, very unusually, she accepted what I was saying and cut back on what she insured. When we got Lottie, this was a subject that had to be addressed, because a dog is not a cat, and the bills can be very high. I mention cats, because we decided from the start that we would not buy insurance for Lulu. As much as we loved her, we are both level-headed enough to accept that if she contracted a serious / potentially fatal condition we would let her go. Better to give another stray cat a home than spend thousands of pounds on the one we've got. To some extent this view, for me, is about what is perhaps an exceptional understanding of the nature of disease and medical treatment. If Lulu got cancer, there would no question of treating it. And I put my money where my mouth is because I have precisely the same policy for myself. My understanding of cancer is that you have some horrendous medical treatment, and then you die. My policy is simply to cut out the middle man.

I only mention this to explain my view of heroic veterinary treatment. The problem, I think, for a lot of people is that they start spending money at perhaps a low level, then things escalate and they are spending more than they bargained for. To use a car analogy, it's like repairing an old car because you think that's all it needs, then another problem comes up and you think, well I've spent money on it now so it doesn't make sense to scrap it, and on you go until one day you realise you've been making bad decisions, that you should have cut and run.

All animals, like all people (and all cars, come to that), are going to die. Medical decisions ought, in my view, to be made based on the value of slowing the dying process. Many years ago, before Liz, Shandy, my long-haired Manchester terrier that we adopted, strangely, in Manchester, had a stroke. She survived that, but then she had another stroke, and another. It wasn't until we saw her wandering around the room bumping into furniture that we realised we had been avoiding our responsibility to end her life in a timely fashion. That was over forty years ago, and to this day I can still clearly remember holding her head while a lovely vet gave her a lethal injection. I should be so lucky.

And shortly before we got Lottie, our cat, George, became more and more sick, and we treated him and sometimes he got better and sometimes he got worse, and then we knew what had to be done. I went with Liz to the vet for it, and to my shame I chickened out and left her holding him while the vet gave him the injection. All I could think of was that every time I had taken him there I had brought him home again, but this time I had betrayed him. I know, it's ridiculous, but I still feel bad about it.

So, did we insure Lottie? Our biggest concern was not terminal disease but injury. Dogs, in my opinion, have legs that are too thin to carry their weight, and they rush around not thinking how fragile they are and how easy it would be to break one. Of course, most dogs never break a leg, which just shows you they might look spindly but they obviously do the job pretty well. Watching Lottie run around, jumping over obstacles, we did worry about that one eventuality. A broken leg is surely not a reason to put a dog down, but on the other hand it will cost thousands of pounds in veterinary bills.

Now, as I mentioned earlier, an insurance company is very good at doing the actuarial calculation, so I did that myself, and on a statistical basis voted against insurance. I fully took Liz's point that statistics are actually nothing more than fairly meaningless numbers, that statistically Lottie was not going to break a leg but in reality it could happen tomorrow. That's a difficult one, because it's that very fear the insurance companies depend on dog owners having. The deciding factor, though, was that we were in a position to underwrite the risk ourselves, which in layman's terms means that if the worst came to the worst we would simply pay the vet ourselves. In short, it was a financial risk that had nothing to do with our relationship with Lottie, because if she broke a leg of course we were going to get it mended for her.

But my cool-headed calculations probably had nothing to do with Liz agreeing not to insure Lottie. The bigger issue had to do with vaccinations. Lottie had the rabies vaccine in Romania, and many of her physiological and psychological problems were reactions to that. I have some specialist knowledge of human immunology, and I am going to assume much of what applies to us also applies to dogs. Any vaccine challenges the immune system – that is in fact its purpose. Rabies is an especially nasty disease, and the vaccine is therefore quite potent in its effect on a dog's immune system. It is of course necessary when moving a dog from one country to another, but the idea that it is a simple, harmless medicine is a fallacy. We give it because we have to but it would be better if we didn't have to. This, as far as I am concerned, militates against importing stray dogs from Romania, but that had not been my decision so there is no point crying over spilt milk.

Once Lottie had had such a serious reaction to the rabies vaccine, giving her any other vaccine was likely to be problematic, because her immune system would remain primed, for ever, to reject vaccines. Now here in the UK, that might not be an issue. Where it does become an issue is if you want to put your dog in a boarding kennel, or take out veterinary insurance. Both require the dog to have annual vaccinations against the common dog viruses, which is quite reasonable. So if Lottie could not have her vaccines, she could not be covered by an insurance policy. There was, therefore, no decision to be made about insurance. It just wasn't possible.

36

Recall

Among the many things that all dogs have which Lottie didn't was recall. I should say all dog owners expect their pet to come when called, and I can understand why they would expect that. Obedience is an important part of dog ownership, and for that reason alone recall matters, but if your dog won't come to you when you call it you are in trouble. You might need to call it more than once, and you might need to inject some sternness into the order, but come what may your dog needs to obey you. Otherwise you lose control, and a dog out of control is a danger to itself and others. If you are in the country, with the dog off lead, and you come to a road, you need to know it will come to you and so avoid danger.

When I say Lottie didn't have recall, I may not have been telling the whole truth, because I have expressed that as being in the past. Truth be told, recall is a skill Lottie has never really learned. She is better than she was at the beginning, but that's not saying a lot. Whether she comes or not is clearly a matter of some indifference to her. She will come if she chooses to, or she has nothing better to do and nowhere better to go, but that's a pretty haphazard state of affairs.

This lack of interest comes, I think, more from her genetic inheritance than anything else. I certainly would not ascribe it to willfulness, which Liz always tended to do. I shouldn't say Lottie is a willful dog, in the human sense (and here we need to be careful not to think she is a four-legged human). I just think she doesn't get the point – that what we want her to do concerns her. She is supremely independent and she has never really taken on board that she is part of a family, and what the family or one of its members wants is something to concern her.

Now all of this is something we could live with. That's not to say we didn't try to coax, encourage and train her to be like other dogs, but we did recognise that trying to get blood out of a stone can be a disappointing exercise. Which raises a question for me. Yes, another question. Why do dogs have recall? I'm not saying Lottie is the only dog in the world that doesn't, but surely most dogs do, and most owners expect them to. Most owners, in fact, would be surprised if their dog did not come when called. But my question is this: why should they? And the second question is: how do they know when their owner wants them to come? And my third question, which might actually be the same as the first question, is: why would they care?

I think the short answer to all of these questions is that dogs relate to their owners. I know that what you say to a dog is irrelevant, that what they respond to is the tone of your voice, so that if you say good dog in a telling-off way they will think they have been told off, and if you say bad dog in a pleased way they will think they are being praised.

Perhaps this is one of the reasons we think dogs are dumb animals, but of course they are only dumb in that they don't speak English, or any other human language. How on Earth can a dog know what we are saying if not by the tone of our voice? So far, so very obvious.

(There is the point that Lottie didn't much care whether we were pleased with her or angry with her. That, as far as she was concerned, was our problem, not hers. Still, most dogs, like most humans, like people to be pleased with them. That's pretty instinctive, the desire to be approved of, in humans and dogs. Not, though, in cats. Cats really could not care less what you think. This may, as I have mentioned before, suggest that Lottie is part cat, but on the other hand it might not.)

I may inadvertently have answered my own question now, which is that dogs want to please their owners, and if their owners say come here they can instinctively tell, or at least they can learn, that coming here is a good thing. When you call your dog and they come, you instinctively reward them with affection, both because you are pleased they have done what you asked and because you love your dog so having it here instead of there is a nice thing, so I suppose it's not hard to see why a dog would learn quite quickly to do that. And here we raise another issue, which is that the dog learns to come to us but we learn that calling them is rewarding not only for them but for us. I have to say that at least in part that teaches us that we can issue an order that will be obeyed. And here the point is, I think, that dog owning is in part rewarding because it gives a creature who does our bidding. That is not a criticism, but it is perhaps an interesting point, that owning a dog is to some extent a nice thing to do because it gives us someone who does what we ask. Anyway, that's venturing into human psychology, which is largely a mystery to me, so perhaps I am straying onto thin ice.

Coming back to my original question, why should a dog care whether it does what we want or not? Well, most people teach their dog to do the basic stuff, like sit and stay. What is the benefit of teaching a dog those things? There probably isn't one, other than what I have just been saying, which is that's an ego trip. We tell ourselves it's good for the dog, but is it? I'm not saying it isn't, I'm just asking the question. OK, dogs do actually seem to get pleasure from doing things. They are intelligent animals, and doing tricks, even basic ones like sit and stay, gives them some kind of reward. But I'm sorry to say this, but is it a real reward or is it a learned reaction to belonging to a human? What I'm trying to ask is, is it a real benefit, or just a benefit that comes out of the relationship between dog and human, but one that actually has no real relevance or importance? It's a circular question, because when wolves became dogs they presumably learned that doing what humans wanted came with benefits, primarily in that they didn't have to hunt for food. Early on in the human / wolf relationship, the humans presumably threw scraps of meat to the animals and the animals learned that sitting waiting for scraps was a lot easier than having to go out and kill something for yourself. I think in those early years wolves and humans learned to hunt together, and wolves, which had been used to hunting in packs, probably learned that hunting with humans could be more successful than hunting with other wolves.

Fast forward to now, and every dog knows that the sound of a tin opener heralds the delivery of food, making them totally dependent on humans. How quickly they would learn to fend for themselves if humans suddenly disappeared, I don't know. It would be interesting to know, but it's an experiment that would require the end of the human race, and that, by definition, would obviate any point in the experiment because we wouldn't be here to see the result, would we?

Anyway, the point I was going to make, as far as I can remember, is that dogs are dependent on their owners, for everything, so pleasing their owners is understood as the quid pro quo for being looked after.

Which brings me back to Lottie. Lottie takes the view that food is her right, whether she works for it or not. She is, as I have said, a lot more like a cat than a dog in that respect.

37

Lottie's Garden

Like any normal dog, Lottie considered the house her territory, once she got over much of her fear and settled down. Where she was most comfortable, though, was in the garden. Once she learned that it was a safe space, she wanted to be out there more than indoors, like most working breeds. And what she wanted more than anything was to sleep out there. We certainly couldn't let her do that, at least not as long as I was living in the house, because foxes visited the back garden at night and that would have caused havoc as she woke all the neighbours.

Strangely, considering her dislike of water, the rain didn't seem to bother her, at least not if it started once she was already settled out there. The thought of her curled up on the patio in the dark and rain wasn't a comfortable one for us, but it was what she wanted. She also liked to make a hollow under one of Liz's bushes to sleep in, whether because it afforded some protection from the rain or some reason we couldn't fathom, there was obviously a reason that worked for her. I don't know if she ever discovered that when she wasn't in it Lulu used it as a toilet, but if she did it didn't seem to bother her.

There were several things that did bother her, and none of them could be avoided. One of them was the elderly man who lived next door, who eccentrically thought it was a good idea to call Lottie from over the fence. She only ever barked at him when he did this, but he never seemed to learn that this was something to do with him. Then there were the seagulls and the squirrels and other casual visitors, all of whom got the sharp end of Lottie's tongue if they invaded her space. And at the end of the garden there was a nursery, the kind that grows children, not plants, and I can tell you children are a lot noisier than plants, which you probably realise. When they came out into the nursery garden, which if you ask me they did more than might be strictly necessary, Lottie went berserk. This was one thing we could do nothing about of course. Actually we could also do nothing about the neighbour and the seagulls, so there was always something for Lottie to get noisy about.

One of my abiding memories of the garden, though, will be the hedgehog hole. We cut a doorway in the fence so that hedgehogs could come and go, which is a good thing to do in any case but it's especially a good thing to do if you are a vegetable gardener, and Liz is an avid one of those, because hedgehogs feed on the slugs that feed on the young vegetables. Liz, being a committed organic gardener, went out at night with a torch to pick the slugs and snails from the lettuces and beans, which I have to say showed admirable perseverance, largely on account of there always being more of them than there were hours of darkness in which to do battle with them.

Anyway, the hedgehog hole also served Lulu as a way in

173

and out of the garden that required less jumping than going over the fence. When our premises were inspected by the charity we got Lottie from, before we were deemed suitable keepers, one of the conditions was that we raise the height of the fence. Don't ask me how high it was, about the same height as most people's fences I should say, but the charity deemed it insufficient for a largish energetic dog bent on escape. Silly people really, because Lottie never tried to escape. Where was she going to go – back to Romania?

Liz wanted to get the fencing people in to attach a trellis all the way round, which was going to cost a lot of money, so I volunteered to save most of that by doing it myself. I've always done a lot of DIY, and I have to say, I'm not very good at it. I always think I can do it but I am almost always disappointed, as are other people. It just seems like the sort of thing a bloke ought to be able to do. Well, this time, I am rather proud to report, I made a pretty good job of it. I thought so, and more importantly Liz thought so, and that's saying something, because she had had experience of my building attempts over the years. Let's face it though, attaching trellis to a fence is hardly a skilled job. We were concerned it was going to spoil the look of the garden but in fact to our surprise it enhanced it.

Lottie was far more interested in sticking her nose through the hedgehog hole than jumping up at the fence, though, and we got used to the sight of her bottom up in the air as she tried to push as much of her head through the hole as she possibly could. I don't know what she thought she was going to see but she spent quite a lot of her time doing it, so I guess there must have been a point.

The garden was an important part of Liz's life, and she had spent a lot of money having it remodelled at one point, which included the installation of five raised beds for her vegetables. Liz was allowed to do stuff with the raised beds, Lulu was allowed to walk on them and use them as a toilet, on account of it being impossible to prevent her, I wasn't allowed near them, but Lottie was another matter. I hardly need say she too was not allowed near them, but the difference between her and me was that I knew what was good for me and Lottie didn't. She was regularly shooed off but by that time she had always done some damage. Telling her off was pointless; you can't go on the raised beds is a meaningless concept to a dog. The raised beds themselves were meaningless to Lottie. How could she tell the difference between being allowed to walk on the path but not the beds? To tell a person not to do something they have to understand what that thing is (even if they don't understand why they can't do it), but of course Lottie was incapable of knowing what they were. It is just one way that exposes the gulf between communicating with a person and doing so with a dog.

I'm afraid here I must wonder about parents who tell their children not to do something, in the mistaken belief their children have any idea what they are talking about. Don't hit your sister sounds obvious to an adult, but is it quite so clear cut to a four-year-old? By the same token, telling a dog to do something, like come here or sit down, is surely more easily understood than telling it not to do something. Not doing is actually a fairly complex concept to a dog. Of course, to a cat it is utterly meaningless, because even if the cat had a clue what you were talking about it wouldn't care. I've been in uniform, so I have a pretty good understanding of what an order means, but a soldier signs up voluntarily to follow orders, making a decision whether he wants to do that or not. A dog has signed up to nothing, so even getting the dog to understand the concept of following an order is problematic. The only hope you've got is that the animal has an instinctive desire to please. Either that or it has learned that when you tell it to do something and it does, you give it a treat for obeying you. So have you trained the dog to obey you to get a treat, or has the dog trained you to give it a treat in return for doing a trick? Perhaps they are not as dumb as they look.

We thought we would never be able to let Lottie sleep out in the garden. Each night I would call her in at bedtime, and each night she would ignore me, and then I would go and find her curled up somewhere and explain that she really did need to come in, and reluctantly she agreed. I always wished I didn't have to make her do it, because it was painfully obvious that she would rather spend the night out there, but what choice did we have?

Then, at some point, I don't know when, it changed. Either the foxes stopped coming into the garden or Lottie stopped worrying about them. On the balance of probabilities I would say it was the former. Perhaps it was necessary for them to learn that a Carpathian Shepherd was on guard there, and the only way they could learn that was if she was, so it seems like they did.

Given her penchant for sleeping in the open air, it will not surprise you that Lottie wasn't keen, when she slept indoors, on spending the whole night on the bed. While Liz was in the bathroom (she always took longer than me to do her ablutions, what with her being a woman probably) if Lottie came up I silently indicated to her that she should jump up. Silently indicating to a dog, as you probably realise, is of limited efficacy, but nevertheless she did sometimes do that, probably because she wanted to rather than because I wanted her to. I knew that whilst Liz would never encourage her to sleep on the bed neither would she tell her to get down. In any case, Lottie never stayed for long, especially if Lulu joined us.

I don't think Lottie had any objection to sleeping on furniture, because her favourite sleeping place in the day was on one of the sofas, either in Liz's office or mine. I assume, therefore, that her objection to sleeping on the bed with us was because we were there. This would be confirmed by the fact that she started to use the bed as yet another of her daytime sleeping places. It would seem that to Lottie people sleeping in the bed was an inconvenience. The same applied, now I think about it, to the sofas. Sometimes, unable to resist, I would lie down with her there, but within a couple of minutes she always got down and moved to the other sofa. I don't think she meant anything personal by it; she just preferred to sleep on her own. If Lulu jumped up and settled next to her, she would usually put up with that, so either she prefers cats to people or she minds small sleeping companions less than large ones.

Coming back to my earlier point, did Lottie want to please us, like most dogs do for their owners? I would have to say no, that was not instinctive in her, and perhaps never will be. This leaves me struggling to explain the relationship, and in any case my relationship with Lottie was different from Liz's. My relationship with Lottie was also different from my relationship with Liz come to that.

Seriously, though, not expecting Lottie to have the instincts we think dogs should have was a large part of how the relationship worked. Being frustrated with her because she wasn't normal was never going to work.

In any case, as she got older Lottie did become more normal. Either that, or we just came to understand her better, so she created her own normality, and what was important was that we let her. Is that, on reflection, much different from human relationships? The person you connect with is never going to be what you want them to be or think they should be, and the relationships that work are, I suppose, therefore, the ones where both parties can adapt to the normality that exists instead of getting frustrated that it's not the one they thought they were getting.

When we chose Lottie from a video online, we almost certainly made lots of assumptions about her, pretty well all of which turned out to be wrong. Do people reject a dog when it turns out not to be what they expected? That probably applies more to rescued dogs than ones that have been paid for, perhaps because rescued dogs are not usually puppies when they are adopted so they have a past, whereas a puppy you can mould in your own image to some extent. And dare I say it, if you have just paid silly money for a puppy you are not likely to hand it over to the RSPCA when the first problem crops up. Sadly, people do, I know, hand back rescued dogs when they find they are unable to cope with them. I wouldn't blame people for that. How many people would have handed Lottie back when they discovered the host of problems she brought with her? I wouldn't blame them if they did. It never occurred to either Liz or me to do that with Lottie, even though at times it was hard. It was Lottie's good fortune, or ours, that we found each other.

38

Decision Time

As the time approached when I knew I was going to have to jump ship, one of the questions that had to be addressed was whether I would be able to take Lottie with me. I knew Liz would not mind; she loved her, but not as much as I did, and she would miss her but not as much as I would. But of course that was only considering us, and what we wanted, but not about what was going to be good for Lottie. It's much the same as what arrangements one has to make for children of a marriage when it comes to an end. The primary concern is not what the parents want but what the children need. You could ask the children, for example, where they want to live, but that would surely be giving them an unfair responsibility.

Anyhow, we couldn't ask Lottie who she wanted to live with, so we had to think ourselves about the issues for her. Although I wanted her more than Liz did, I realised she would be unable, even if we could communicate with her on this, to make that kind of decision. Like a child, she would of course want us to stay together, but there are times in your life when you have to do things you really don't want to do. In a separation, there are no winners, only losers, and yet it has to be done, and everyone concerned has to pay the price. Some couples stay together for the children, and some probably regret that and I expect some don't, but Liz and I were not going to stay together for Lottie's sake, as much as we loved her. As I say, this just had to be done.

On balance, it made sense for her to stay with Liz, because that was her home. She might pretend that she wasn't interested in Lulu, but even the cat, I thought, was part of what made it home for Lottie. Taking her away from everything she knew could not be good for her, and it had to be remembered that the house had, for the past two years, become her territory. We humans can move house, and maybe we do that gladly and maybe we do it with regrets, but how can we know what a house means to a dog that has made it its territory? Yes, of course, if you move house your dog goes with you and it works all right, but this wasn't the case here. Staying in her house was an option, and really it was the only option.

In any case, there were other issues. I was going out into the unknown, and the unknown is not good for any dog, and it was especially not good for Lottie, who had survived and thrived at least in part because of the stability we had given her. And since I was going to rent a house, it was inevitable that in her lifetime I would move more than once, whereas Liz was never going to leave her house. And then, when I did find the house I was going to move to, the final straw was that it was a cottage on a farm, and because of the livestock there the lease prohibited the keeping of a dog. In a way, it was a bit of a relief, because it wasn't me saying she couldn't come with me.

39

The End

And so I come to the end. Not the end for Lottie or for me, but the end of this book. I hope I have entertained you, which I trust I do with everything I write, especially my novels, but specifically I hope my story of Lottie has resonated with you.

Mostly, though, I hope for my beloved dog that she has done the one thing I cannot do. I cannot forget her, but I hope she has forgotten me. I had to leave my children when my first marriage ended, and I cannot ever forgive myself for that, and I'm afraid I cannot quite forgive myself for leaving Lottie. For the first weeks and months, I knew she was waiting for me to come back, because I had gone on trips before but I had come back. Like me, she will have got on with her life, because there was no choice. I can only hope and pray that she got over the separation, and that she has the thing I have talked about so much in this book.

Happiness.

I can't have a dog, but I have a car called Rover.

If you find any errors in this book, don't be shy,
let me know:

robert@brynin.com

Printed in Great Britain
by Amazon